ancient paths

Discover Christian Formation
the Benedictine Way

DAVID ROBINSON

PARACLETE PRESS
BREWSTER, MASSACHUSETTS

Ancient Paths: Discover Christian Formation the Benedictine Way

Copyright © 2010 by David Robinson

ISBN: 978-1-55725-773-4

Library of Congress Cataloging-in-Publication Data

Robinson, David, 1957-

  Ancient paths : discover Christian formation the Benedictine way.

     p. cm.

  Includes bibliographical references.

  ISBN 978-1-55725-773-4

  1. Benedict, Saint, Abbot of Monte Cassino. Regula. 2. Spiritual life—Christianity. 3. Spiritual formation. I. Title.

  BX3004.Z5R58 2010

  248.4--dc22   2010013782

10 9 8 7 6 5 4 3 2 1

Published by Paraclete Press

Brewster, Massachusetts

www.paracletepress.com

Printed in the United States of America

CONTENTS

PREFACE   vii

INTRODUCTION *Which Way Will We Go?*   xi

PART ONE

ANCIENT PERSPECTIVES ON CHRISTIAN FORMATION

1. *How Benedict Transformed the World*   3

2. *Benedictine Essentials for the Journey*   18

3. *The Path of Communal Prayer*   41

4. *The Path of Spiritual Guidance*   56

5. *The Path of Ordinary Spirituality*   76

6. *The Path of* Lectio Divina   92

7. *The Path of Hospitality*   109

PART TWO

CHRISTIAN FORMATION AS A WAY OF LIFE TOGETHER

8. *How Benedict Is Still Transforming the World*   129

9. *Five Case Studies of Christian Formation*   152

10. *A Guide for Christian Formation in a Local Church*   172

11. *User's Guide to Going on a Monastic Retreat*   182

12. *A Year of Tools for Christian Formation*   198

AFTERWORD *Guidance on Ancient Paths*   204

ACKNOWLEDGMENTS   209

APPENDIX *Twelve-Week Study Guide for* Ancient Paths   211

NOTES   221

SELECTED BIBLIOGRAPHY   231

In October 1986, when I made my first monastic retreat to Our Lady of Guadalupe Trappist Abbey, near Lafayette, Oregon, I had only been ordained as a Minister of Word and Sacrament in the Presbyterian Church for two years and was serving as pastor to the people of Smith Memorial Presbyterian Church, Fairview, Oregon. After two short years in my new profession, I was discouraged, weary of ministry, and looking for guidance in my vocation as a pastor. My senior pastor, Slider Steuernol, made his first monastic retreat to Our Lady of Guadalupe in the summer of 1986. He encouraged me to get away for a weeklong monastic retreat. Since I was on the verge of burnout and soon to leave my position as a pastor in Fairview, a week at a monastery was a welcomed gift for renewal and discernment.

Like all monasteries based upon *The Rule of St. Benedict*, Our Lady of Guadalupe Trappist Abbey welcomed me that autumn like a lost son come home. By God's grace, during that week I began my lifelong journey into contemplative Christian formation. Since that first retreat, I've returned to Guadalupe Abbey many times, and also made retreats and visits to dozens of other monasteries that live according to Benedictine principles. I also began to read and study *The Rule of St. Benedict* and discovered the wisdom and beauty of this way of living, as I sought to apply monastic spirituality to my daily life. In October 2005, I enrolled in Fuller Theological Seminary's Doctor of Ministry in Christian Spirituality program to formally study Christian formation, from both historical and practical perspectives. Five months later, in February 2006, I became a Benedictine Oblate with Mount Angel Abbey in Mount Angel, Oregon, by making a lifelong commitment to practice Benedictine spirituality as much as possible within my station in life. I continue to make annual retreats to Benedictine monasteries, seeking to grow in my understanding and practice of Christian formation.

That first monastic retreat in 1986 seemed to me like stepping through a gate into an expansive and beautiful park. Since the 1990s, our family has hiked hundreds of miles in the heart of Olympic National Park, a wonderland of beauty on the Olympic peninsula in Washington State. Like our annual family hikes in this park, over the course of the past two decades, my exploration in the "park" of Benedictine spirituality has deeply shaped my life and faith, helping me to become more and more like Christ. In the pages below, I describe this life as walking together along "ancient paths." Since my first encounter with St. Benedict and his *Rule* in 1986, I've become much more intentional about Christian formation, seeking the best ways to grow together with Christ's family, the church. Year after year, new habits have been birthed by putting monastic ways into practice in my own life and, with others, in the life of the local church.

I owe a debt of gratitude to the people of Community Presbyterian Church, Cannon Beach, for their faithful support and love. Since 1993, when we first arrived in Cannon Beach, I've been encouraged to grow in my understanding and practice of Christian formation in this family of faith. Over the past seventeen years, I've seen members of this congregation grow and flourish in their love of Christ as we've sought to live according to the principles laid out in the following pages. The vision statement of Community Presbyterian Church, "seeking to know Christ and grow in Christ together," lies at the heart of all Christian formation. I invite you to explore with me *The Rule of St. Benedict*, to discover wisdom and refreshment for your daily life of faith in your journey with the Lord. In reading this book, may you be encouraged to know Christ and grow closer to Christ as you walk with others along paths of Benedictine spirituality.

Which Way Will We Go?

This is what the LORD says: "Stand at the crossroads and look;
ask for the ancient paths, ask where the good way is, and walk
in it, and you will find rest for your souls. But you said, 'We
will not walk in it.'"

—JEREMIAH 6:16

Thou my everlasting portion, more than friend or life to me,
All along my pilgrim journey, Savior, let me walk with thee.
Close to thee, close to thee, close to thee, close to thee,
All along my pilgrim journey, Savior, let me walk with thee.

—FANNY CROSBY

Benedict of Nursia (ca. 480–547)
stood at the crossroads of the early sixth century, looking for
guidance along the way of Christ. The way he chose led him
into Christian life in community. Along this way, St. Benedict
not only found rest for his soul but also helped millions of
others discover "the good way," the way of transformation
through Jesus Christ and Christian community. The guidebook

St. Benedict wrote for formation in community, known as *The Rule of St. Benedict*, has been the source of daily guidance for millions of believers living in Christian community. *The Rule of St. Benedict* has guided the daily lives of monks around the world for fifteen centuries, but also has offered nonmonastic Christians guidance for Christian formation in community.

Why look to a monk who lived so long ago for guidance in the way of Christ? Isn't the Bible a sufficient source of truth and counsel? The Bible is our foundation for truth, authority, and wisdom in living as followers of Jesus Christ. That is exactly what makes Benedict's *Rule* such a practical and enduring book, for he founded his guidebook in Christ and in Scripture. Along with many other great resources from church history, this sixth-century guidebook has been rediscovered and studied anew in the past few decades, offering a whole new generation of people direction as they stand at the crossroads of this new century. Though I'm neither a monk nor a Roman Catholic, I too have discovered *The Rule of St. Benedict* to be a reliable guidebook for formation in the community of the local church.

Just as there are many paths through a forest, there are also many ways of spirituality. My undergraduate degree was in comparative world religion (University of Washington, Seattle, 1979); studying for this degree helped me better understand the diversity of approaches to belief among people of faith around the world. Likewise, among Christians, there are many ways of living by faith in Christ. These diverse ways of formation beautifully express the creativity and wonder of Christ's life in all his glory and wisdom. Yet, there are also some ways of living that fall far short of Christ's way of life and love. Consider, for a moment, three such alternative paths to spirituality found among Christians today: private spirituality, antinomian spirituality, and nomadic spirituality.

Many believe faith to be a private matter; something so near to the heart that it is impossible to express in words. As I was growing up, I was warned against "wearing religion on your sleeve"—another way of saying it is that it is better to keep all matters of faith and religion to myself. When faith is viewed primarily as private, we become isolated from other Christians, and tend to hide the treasure of faith given to us by Christ. The way of private spirituality leads people into a solo journey of faith in Christ, often with little or no connection with other believers. In Benedict's day, such solo travelers were known as *anchorites*, or hermits, from two Greek words, *anachoreo*, "living apart," and *eremos*, "solitary." The solitary way of life spread during the fourth century through the widely popular *Life of St. Anthony*, a biography of the Desert Father Anthony of Egypt, written by Athanasius (296–373), the bishop of Alexandria. Though the solitary way of life was accepted by the early church as a potential life's calling for a Christian, and also as an occasional retreat for times of renewal, it was not considered a normative lifestyle for followers of Christ. The solitary way of faith is quite common today. Some followers of Christ in the twenty-first century would rather walk alone, seeing spirituality as a private journey unencumbered by the hassles and demands of human community. As evidenced in media and marketing, contemporary culture often elevates the individual above the community. This is nothing new to our time. Every generation has flirted with traveling solo.

Certainly, the Christian way of life is both individual and communal. There are aspects of solitary spirituality that are essential to inner growth. For example, prayer is both something we practice alone, and something we share with others. We are wise to keep a creative tension between individual and communal perspectives in understanding Christian formation. What Benedict warns us against is the avoidance of community and the excessive emphasis upon private spirituality that precludes the support of Christian community. He affirmed the solitary life of the hermit as appropriate for the spiritually mature, yet he also believed hermits needed to be connected to the wider community of faith. According to Benedict, the solo journey of faith belongs only to those who have "built up their strength and go from the battle line in the ranks of their brothers to the single combat of the desert. Self-reliant now, without the support of another, they are ready with God's help to grapple single-handed with the vices of body and mind" (RB, 1.5). Generally, we need the support of other believers in order to grow in Christ.

A second unhealthy path, according to the *Rule*, is the antinomian way, or the "feel good" way, of spirituality. Just as in Benedict's day, there are many today who center their lives upon feelings and intuitions, looking to inner experience as the most reliable guide for personal growth. Some believers today avoid external laws, rules, and structures, and see these as obstacles to personal maturity. There is nothing wrong with feeling good about life, but Benedict warns against those who discard rules and supervision for their life of faith and choose to live instead without any outside guidance to govern their lives. According to Benedict, "with no experience to guide them, no rule to try them *as gold is tried in a furnace* (Prov. 27:21)" they find their life ruled by "whatever strikes their fancy" (RB, 1.8). The Christian life involves both an inner and an outer aspect. There is a creative balance between structure and spirit—between law and grace in Christian formation. Jesus warned against blind conformity to the law without any regard for the spirit. Paul declared that the letter of the law kills whereas the Spirit of God brings life (see 2 Cor. 3:6). Mere conformity to external laws and regulations, without regard for a personal relationship with God's Spirit, leads to lifeless faith. On the other hand, when authority and laws are discarded, we too easily allow our own feelings to become our authority rather than the Word of God. Without wise spiritual leadership and accountability in community, we can more easily drift into idolatry or self-worship, and place ourselves instead of Christ in the role of authority over our spiritual lives. "Anything they believe in and choose, they call holy; anything they dislike, they consider forbidden" (RB, 1.9). The way of Christ calls us into a life of formation in which we willingly choose to be guided by Christ through Scripture and by wise leadership in community.

A third type of unhealthy spirituality commonly found in Benedict's day, as well as in our own time, is nomadic spirituality. In the sixth century, as in every age, there were nomadic, wandering believers who claimed no home or community. People of faith still choose to live with little or no commitment to the local church. After living on the Oregon coast for seventeen years, I'm still amazed how often I meet believers with no spiritual home. One of the frequent pictures Jesus used to describe life with God is a plant with roots. Much of the health and fruitfulness of a person's spirituality depends upon the roots. Without any roots in a faith community, some believers become uprooted, restlessly moving, seldom settling down for any length of time. Benedict described such people in his day as those who "spend their entire lives drifting from region to region. . . . Always on the move, they never settle down, and are slaves to their own wills and gross appetites" (RB, 1.10–11). Nomadic Christians move from place to place, from church to church, seldom settling down or planting roots. Of course, Christianity is also a faith that calls us to go into the world and make disciples. Jesus assumed his followers would be mobile, bringing the Good News to all nations. Christian formation requires both mobility and stability. In the first decade of the twenty-first century, there seems to be a high value placed upon mobility, often at the expense of stability. Due to the pursuit of better housing and employment, people frequently move from city to city, from job to job, and thus, from church to church. A common condition today is a sense of being spiritually homeless and personally disconnected from others. According to a Gallup poll taken in May 2007, 86 percent of Americans claim to pray to God, while only 31 percent claim to attend a weekly church worship service. This gap suggests there are millions of pilgrims who remain aloof from other Christians in their area and have no place to call their spiritual home.

The *Rule* warns against each of these three unhealthy alternatives, inviting followers of Christ to walk in a new way. Benedictine formation is a journey that begins with a commitment to three lifelong promises:

- Stability in community
- Fidelity in community
- Obedience in community

"When he is to be received, he comes before the whole community . . . and promises stability, fidelity to monastic life, and obedience" (RB, 58.17). These three Benedictine promises or vows offer an antidote to the three unhealthy ways listed above. The way of stability provides a safe home for those tired of nomadic spirituality. The way of fidelity in community cuts to the heart of private spirituality. The way of obedience keeps challenging antinomian spirituality. Among the many alternative patterns for spiritual life, how can we know which way is the good way? In Benedict's vision, growth occurs relationally, as we journey together in Christ united in a life of stability, fidelity, and obedience in community.

The prophet Jeremiah called out to his generation to walk upon the path of the Lord. "Stand at the crossroads and look; ask for the ancient paths, ask where the good way is, and walk in it, and you will find rest for your souls" (6:16). Eleven centuries later, Benedict called out to his generation to stand at the crossroads, look for the good way, and walk together as a people of faith on "ancient paths." There are those in our generation who are looking for wise guidebooks that offer principles as well as practical wisdom for the spiritual journey. As a guidebook, the *Rule* has offered sound guidance for hundreds of thousands of pilgrims, guiding them on their spiritual journey in Christ. The *Rule* was not written in a monastic vacuum, but rather as a daily handbook for the formation of faith in the community at the Abbey of Monte Cassino in Italy. After fifteen centuries, the *Rule* still offers a daily guide for living together as followers of Jesus Christ. Monks in Benedictine communities who live their daily lives based upon *The Rule of St. Benedict* include the Order of Saint Benedict (OSB), the Order of Cistercians (O.CIST.), the Order of Cistercians of the Strict Observance (OCSO), also known as Trappists, and the Anglican Benedictines.

In addition, many nonmonastics have also turned to the *Rule* in contemporary times, discovering a wise guidebook for Christian formation outside the walls of the monastery. Worldwide, a growing number of nonmonastic people are seeking to live their daily lives according to the *Rule*, including those known as Benedictine Oblates or associates. The international community of Benedictine Oblates includes almost twenty-five thousand men and women around the world, people who daily seek to live according to the Benedictine way of faith within their station of life. These Benedictine Oblates, along with thousands of other pilgrims, are discovering the *Rule* as a guidebook full of practical wisdom for travelers, offering precisely the kind of guidance needed for formation in local congregations in the twenty-first century.

As we stand at the crossroads in our time, who will point us in the right direction? Which way will we go? I've written this book to introduce you to Benedict and his guidebook for the journey of Christian formation. How can busy, active people find rest for their souls and guidance for the pilgrimage of faith that lies ahead? Come along paths of Christian spirituality and discover an ancient way of faith practiced within Christian communities around the world for more than a thousand years. Across the centuries, Benedict continues to call people into a lifelong pilgrimage of faith: "See how the Lord in his love shows us the way of life. Clothed then with faith and the performance of good works, let us set out on this way, with the Gospel for our guide" (RB, prologue 20–21).

PART ONE

ANCIENT PERSPECTIVES
ON CHRISTIAN FORMATION

CHAPTER 1

How Benedict Transformed the World

As a pastor of a local church, I receive numerous mail and e-mail solicitations every month, offering new ministry strategies that include church growth seminars, leadership webcasts, mission conferences, faith curriculum, or worship media tools. With the advent of the Internet, instant global communication, and jet airplane travel, the options available to pastors and churches to participate in such events can be overwhelming: Which model for church growth would work best in our situation? Where should I go for wisdom concerning Christian formation? What resources will help us grow as a church? I've struggled with such questions over my quarter of a century as an ordained minister. Through all the conferences and seminars I've attended, and in all the books I've read, and all the research I've done, I haven't found a better guide for Christian formation than *The Rule of St. Benedict.*

The following pages offer a biblical approach to Christian formation for the twenty-first century by drawing upon a field-tested guidebook. In this chapter I would like to introduce you to the author of this guidebook and show how he transformed the world through his remarkable *Rule.* In chapter two, we will survey Benedictine essentials for the journey of faith. Then, step-by-step, through the next five chapters, we will journey together through the villages of Benedictine spirituality, exploring five paths of Christian formation. As you better understand Benedict's life and spiritual practices, I hope you will be better equipped to implement his practical vision in your personal life and in your local church and be better able to carry out Christ's world-transforming ways through your daily life.

THE LIFE AND TIMES OF BENEDICT OF NURSIA

Benedict of Nursia was born into a collapsing civilization. The late fifth and early sixth centuries were marked by widespread societal turmoil that included political corruption, military invasions, and ecclesiastical crises. Though the Roman Empire had ruled over a vast territory for five centuries, by the late fifth century the administration of Rome had fallen into decline. Sickened by internal corruption and poorly managed government, Rome was eroding from the inside while being attacked from the outside. Tribal armies from the north and the east invaded down the spine of Italy with increasing frequency, leaving people in constant fear of invasion, famine, and disease. Seven decades before the birth of Benedict, in 410, the city of Rome was overthrown by the Goths under the command of Alaric. In 455, Rome was once again sacked, this time by Vandals from North Africa. In 476, just four years before Benedict's birth, the boy-emperor Romulus was deposed by barbarian leaders.

Benedict was born around 480, in Nursia, an Italian town now called Norcia, nestled in the Sabine mountains, a little north of Rome. His twin sister, Scholastica, also became a monastic, founding a convent that carries her name to this day. As a teenager Benedict was sent to Rome to receive a classical education. While studying in Rome, Benedict witnessed the diversions and temptations of city life. As his first biographer, Gregory the Great, wrote:

> During his boyhood [Benedict] showed mature understanding, and
> a strength of character far beyond his years kept his heart detached
> from every pleasure. Even while still living in the world, free to
> enjoy all it had to offer, he saw how empty it was and turned from
> it without regret. . . . In his desire to please God alone, he turned
> his back on further studies.

As a young student, Benedict renounced the culture of Rome, fled
the company of humans, and walked eastward along footpaths into
the Italian mountain wilderness, to a place known as Subiaco, in the
valley of the Anio River. Here he lived in a solitary cave. Benedictine
historian Jean Leclercq, OSB, offers this answer to the possible reasons
why Benedict left Rome:

> Why? Not because he was doing poorly in his studies—that is not
> implied at all—but because student life, school life, is full of danger to
> morals. All the rest of St. Benedict's life was to be subordinated to the
> search for God, and lived out under the best conditions for reaching
> that goal, that is to say, in separation from this dangerous world. Thus,
> in the life of St. Benedict, we find, in germ, the two components of
> monastic culture: studies undertaken, and then, not precisely scorned,
> but renounced and transcended, for the sake of the kingdom of God.

Fed by a local monk who regularly lowered bread on a rope down
the steep cliff to the mouth of his cave, Benedict spent his first few
years as a hermit, and committed himself to the ascetic disciplines
of silence, solitude, and prayer.

After a time, monks from the neighboring town recognized
Benedict to be a holy man of prayer and asked him to become their

community leader. He reluctantly agreed, calling these men into a disciplined way of life, a common life together within a daily rhythm of work, sacred reading, and prayer. During the next two decades, Benedict worked out his understanding of Christian formation within the laboratory of the monastery. When more men joined the fledgling movement, Benedict organized his monks into groups of twelve and placed a director over each house. He himself served as leader over all the houses. Not all these monks were pleased with Benedict's approach to life in community. They attempted to poison him on two separate occasions. Benedict left the area of Subiaco with a number of loyal monks. This small community of monks walked southward to a mountaintop—the site of a ruined pagan temple.

> Almost half-way between Rome and Naples, the Via Latina, which connects these two cities, skirts this steep and prominent mountain. A little above the level of the valley, close to the rocky wall, nestles the fortified town of Casinum, now San Germano. From there a path winds upwards to a height of some two thousand feet above, where it ends even today in the imposing remains of an ancient pelasgic fortress, which in the olden times crowned the summit of the rock.

There on the heights of Monte Cassino, Benedict founded a new monastery in 529 and there he wrote his *Regula*, known today as *The Rule of St. Benedict*.

The Latin word he chose as the title for his work, *Regula*, means yardstick, or measuring tool. One of the difficulties in our shared life in Christ concerns how to measure or evaluate spiritual growth within a faith community. An overreliance upon measuring tools can lead to legalism that cripples growth. On the other hand, abandonment of all measuring tools can lead to a lack of accountability that also stifles growth. Benedict offered a middle way, emphasizing the importance within a faith community of *regula*, or measuring tools. He wrote a communal guidebook to help assess and nurture spiritual growth within a Christian community. In this book, I refer to this work as the *Rule*, and I will keep in step with Benedict's journey metaphor by referring to his *Rule* as a guidebook for our journey together.

Benedict composed the *Rule* to guide the daily journey of the monks at the Abbey of Monte Cassino. Today, people of all Christian backgrounds turn to its wisdom for practical guidance in living for Christ in community. The majority of such people today are not monks, but laypeople, active in daily vocations in the world. This would come as no surprise to Benedict of Nursia. While he had a high regard for the vocation of the priesthood, he apparently remained a layperson throughout his vocation as a monk. The *Rule* is flavored by a moderate, commonsense voice of a layperson, with only a few references to priests, a few implied references to the sacraments, and very little attention paid to the ecclesiastical structures of the church. One Benedictine scholar explains: "To the modern reader, the scarcity of references to the Eucharist in the [*Rule of Benedict*] may seem scandalous. The term *eucharistia* never appears. . . . The liturgical code . . . makes no references at all to Mass." Over the centuries, life within the Benedictine cloister developed a complex ecclesiastical and sacramental system that the founder of the order would have found unusual. Benedict's community was centered upon Christ, the Scriptures, and the daily life of prayer and work in community.

Benedict founded one other monastery in southern Italy before he died at nearly seventy years of age in 547. The statue of the saint in the cloister garden at the Abbey of Monte Cassino, titled *Dying Benedict*, depicts him at the time of his death, standing with face and hands raised to heaven, supported by monks on either side, offering his life and soul to Christ. As he wrote in the second to last chapter of the *Rule*, so he lived to his dying breath: "Let them prefer nothing whatever to Christ, and may he bring us all together to everlasting life" (RB, 72.11).

HOW BENEDICT TRANSFORMED THE WORLD

According to historian W.H.C. Frend, "Benedictine monasticism spread slowly. By the end of the sixth century it still seems to have been unknown outside Italy." The early champion of Benedict and his *Rule* was his first biographer, Gregory the Great (540–604), who published *Life and Miracles of St. Benedict* just fifty years after Benedict's death. By the time Gregory became pope in 590, the political disorder throughout the Roman Empire had spread such unrest and suffering that people increasingly turned to the church and to the abbey for help rather than to the government of Rome. Gregory was himself a monk, with strong affinities toward Benedict's vision of monastic life. Thanks to the support and missionary vigor of Gregory the Great during his fourteen years as pope, the *Rule* and Benedictine monasticism began to be spread across Europe. In 595, Gregory commissioned Augustine, a Sicilian monk, to go as a missionary to Britain. Along with a small group of other monks, Augustine arrived at Canterbury in the kingdom of Kent in 597, carrying with him the sacred Scriptures and *The Rule of St. Benedict*. "At Canterbury Augustine began a monastery," relates church historian Kenneth Latourette, "using a pagan temple which had been given him by the King. Following the Benedictine rule, [Canterbury] became the prototype of many Benedictine houses in England."

Over the next century, the *Rule* gradually took root in the soil of Britain, governing the life of many monasteries, including those under the leadership of such influential abbots as St. Wilfrid of Ripon, York (634–709), and St. Benedict Biscop (628–90), founder of Monkwearmouth and Jarrow in the north of England. After the Synod of Whitby in 664 and the Synod at Autun in 670, *The Rule of St. Benedict* became the normative monastic rule in much of Britain and Gaul. During the next five centuries, hundreds of Benedictine abbeys were established throughout Britain and across the European continent.

In the early ninth century, during the fourteen-year reign of Emperor Charlemagne, Benedict of Aniane (750–821), sometimes called "the second St. Benedict," adopted a strict observance of the *Rule* in his monastery in southern France. Benedict, having served earlier both in the military and in the court of Charlemagne, during which time he became a monk, was now called upon by Charlemagne to lead a monastic reform in his region of France according to his strict observance of the *Rule.* "The wide dissemination of St. Benedict's Rule," asserts author Edwin Mullins, "is largely due to Charlemagne and the scholars of his court, men with a reverence for antique knowledge and the desire to find and copy the original texts of the early church." The oldest surviving copy of the *Rule*, "the famous manuscript preserved for many centuries at St. Gall or Sankt Gallen, the Codex Sangallensis," is thought to have been a copy of the original manuscript of *The Rule of St. Benedict*, kept in Rome after Benedict's death. Codex Sangallensis 914, dating to 810, during the reign of Charlemagne, is accepted as the most authoritative surviving manuscript of the *Rule.* "It remains a faithful copy," declares Cambridge medievalist Christopher Brooke, "made by Carolingian scholars, from a model very close to Benedict's own text, still close enough to mirror the degenerate spelling and syntax of sixth-century Latin much more faithfully than the copies to which we are used to today."

After the death of Charlemagne in 814, Louis the Pious, Charlemagne's son, continued his father's plans for monastic reforms by calling a series of synods to be held in Aachen. "Louis made Benedict of Aniane his adviser on monastic affairs, and the order went forth that all monasteries in the realm must follow the Benedictine rule as interpreted by him." This order, the fruit of the Synod of Aachen in 817, declared *The Rule of St. Benedict* the standard monastic rule on the continent. Louis also appointed Benedict of Aniane the archabbot of all the monasteries of Francia, the region we now know as France.

One of the most influential of these French Benedictine abbeys from that medieval era was the Abbey of Cluny in southern Burgundy, founded in 910. Like the monastic reforms of the ninth century, the Cluniac reform of Benedictine monasticism in the tenth century returned monasteries to a strict observance of the *Rule*. The founder of Cluny, William, Duke of Aquitaine, also took the bold step of centralizing power in the motherhouse with the abbot of Cluny accountable directly to the pope. "Cluny's abbots," declares Mullins, "were as influential as any president, statesmen, or business leader in our own times." The early abbots of Cluny offered spiritual and ecclesiastical leadership to emperors, popes, dukes, and dignitaries across the European continent. As the Cluniac movement spread across the continent, the *Rule* also spread, bringing Benedictine gifts of literacy, libraries, health care, economic development, and above all, hundreds of missional communities of praying monks. By the end of the twelfth century, the Cluniac order claimed fifteen hundred dependent monasteries with over ten thousand monks spread across

France, Germany, Spain, Italy, and Britain. Each monastery reported directly to Cluny under a hierarchical structure of ecclesiastical government previously unknown in Benedictine circles.

Another significant medieval Benedictine reform movement began in Citeaux, France, in 1098. Founded by Robert of Molesmes, the abbey at Citeaux, motherhouse to the Cistercian order, exemplified a connectional approach to ecclesiastical government. The Cistercian movement of Benedictine monasticism allowed each individual abbey to govern its own internal affairs, yet connected abbeys together through an informal fraternal network. Annually, each Cistercian abbey sent a delegate to Citeaux to discuss issues related to monastic life. Bernard of Clairvaux became abbot of Citeaux in 1112, just fourteen years after this new monastery had been founded. After three years, Bernard was sent by Abbot Stephen to found another monastic house in the Champagne region of France. Bernard called his newly formed abbey *Clairvaux*, or "valley of light." Bernard was to have a major influence upon European history as a Benedictine monk through his preaching, his writings, and his dynamic approach to leadership. As a Benedictine leader, Bernard further spread Benedict's legacy of spiritual vision and daily practice of the Christian life in community in the West.

The profound influence of Benedict and the *Rule* may be observed from various points of view: geography, culture, education, health care, economics, and spirituality. By the eve of the Reformation in the early sixteenth century, Benedictine communities across Europe numbered in the thousands. Not a single square mile of land in all Europe was more than a day's ride on horseback from the nearest Benedictine monastery. In the early 1500s, Benedictine, Cluniac, or Cistercian abbeys were found in every corner of Europe—the most northern climates of the Scandinavian countries, the eastern regions of the European continent, the Mediterranean coastlands of southern Europe, the westernmost islands of Britain, and in every province and region in between. Through the genius of the *Rule*, Benedict offered civilization an enduring and sustainable way of life that was transportable and adaptable to a wide variety of languages, ethnicities, and climates.

Benedict dramatically transformed European art, literature, and architecture by encouraging the practice of the arts in the monastery. Every Benedictine monastery housed a thriving cottage industry of artisans who created some of the outstanding works of art in the medieval period. Thousands of monasteries across Europe acted as local art centers and developed methods and approaches to such a diversity of art forms as calligraphy, illuminated manuscripts, painting, glassworks, architecture, sculpture, masonry, winemaking, barrel craft, furniture design, weaving, music composition, and liturgical drama. The creativity and craftsmanship developed within the Benedictine abbey strongly influenced the rise of the artisan guilds of Europe and eventually even assisted in the development of the middle class and the marketplace where such crafts were bought and sold.

Benedict's world-changing educational legacy began with his conviction that every monk, regardless of class or status, must learn to read. By the time of the Cluniac reform, every Benedictine monastery housed a library and a scriptorium, where monks copied and archived the great manuscripts of antiquity, including thousands of Bible manuscripts from the early centuries of the fledgling Christian movement. Through the daily monastic discipline of reading, especially of the sacred reading of Scripture, Benedict greatly impacted the literacy of the West. The development of libraries, the preservation of classic works of antiquity, and the rise of an international system of education across the European continent all have their foundations during the medieval period in the Benedictine cloister. The first universities of the West arose from monasteries and cathedrals. The first words people learned to read were from manuscripts copied by monks. The finest education offered to a continent for the thousand years prior to the Reformation was to be found in a Benedictine monastery. This was no small accomplishment during an era commonly known as the Dark Ages, when illiteracy was the norm, poverty was widespread, and education was the exclusive privilege of the wealthy.

Benedictine practices also transformed the world of health care. Though the monasteries of Europe were primarily designed as places of prayer and worship, every abbey also included both an infirmary and a guest house where local citizens could come to find rest or physical cures for their illnesses. Thanks to the inquisitive minds of monks and nuns, new treatments were developed through the centuries to help cure the ailments of residents of the monastery and of the neighboring towns. An example of such medical advances in the medieval period is Benedictine abbess Hildegard of Bingen (1098–1179), known not only for her extraordinary musical compositions, visionary theological writings, hundreds of letters to popes and kings, but also for her writings on natural history and her book of physical cures. Following in Benedict's footsteps, Hildegard developed new medicines and cures among the Benedictine sisters of the twelfth century—pioneering the practice of homeopathic and herbal medicine, hundreds of years before these medical arts would become widely accepted in the West. Through the stability of the Benedictine abbey, local citizens could receive medical help. Many monasteries developed into hospitals, hospice houses for the dying, and care centers for the practice of the healing arts. The impact of Benedictine health care was dramatically felt in England when from 1536 to 1540, King Henry

VIII closed over 800 monasteries, thereby taking away thousands of hospital beds across the country. Though several monastic hospitals in London were appropriated by King Henry VIII after 1540 including St. Bartholomew's, St. Thomas's, and Bethlehem Hospital, the rest of the country would wait another two hundred years for the return of charitable health care with the rise of voluntary hospitals in the mid-1700s.

Benedict also profoundly impacted the economic development of the West. The phrase *ora et labora*, or "pray and work," summarizes Benedictine spirituality: the warp and woof tapestry of the life of prayer and the physical life of manual labor. Monks were to consider their work, whether prayer or plowing, as an act of devotion to God. This singular vision of work enhanced the work ethic of the monastery, improved the quality of labor, and sustained the monastery through the development of cottage industries. Every monk took a vow of stability, a commitment to the community, to the abbot, and to the *Rule*. As a result, abbeys became stable economic communities with a long-range vision for developing orchards and vineyards, draining swamps and other local land improvements for production of agriculture, constructing irrigation systems to bring water into the monastic community, and improving roads to enhance trading the goods raised in the monastery. For example, one of the first projects at Citeaux was to provide adequate water to the swampy monastic grounds. The monks spent ten years digging a canal from a spring ten miles away to supply sufficient water for the community. On my visit to Citeaux in 2005, I witnessed the water flowing in abundance from the same spring accessed by Cistercian monks nine centuries earlier. Over time, local citizens recognized the abbeys as reliable sources of quality labor, goods, and commerce. With the economic stability of the Benedictine cloister, people were drawn into the regions where abbeys were founded.

Over the centuries, villages and towns sprang up in the vicinity of Benedictine monasteries across the European continent. Over the course of the first millennium after Benedict's death, abbeys were instrumental in the development of European architecture, agriculture, infrastructure of roads and waterways, literacy, artistic culture, health care, and economic growth. The *Rule*, as lived out daily in monasteries through the centuries, played an enormous role in shaping European civilization during the medieval period of history. As Edwin Mullins writes,

> In those distant days it was the monasteries that held a vital key to the shaping of a new Europe. They acted as colleges, patrons of art and architecture, moral guardians, benevolent landlords, founders of social services, centers of capital wealth, as well as being institutions of vast political influence on an international scale, with the ear of kings, emperors, and popes.

BENEDICTINE FORMATION

Beyond mere geographic, cultural, educational, medical, or economic development, the greatest impact of the Benedictine movement springs from the original vision for spiritual formation in community. From the heights of Monte Cassino in Italy, Benedict offered the world new vistas on Christian formation. The genius of his perspective on life together is first discovered in his understanding of the place of vows in shaping the life of a community. Drawing upon the richness of the past, Benedict formulated new vows to join the classical vow of obedience. Uniting the vows of poverty and chastity into a new single vow of fidelity or "conversion of life" (*conversatione morum*;

RB, 58.17), Benedict included a new vow of stability, something that "proved to be among the real strengths of the movement." Through a commitment to stability, fidelity, and obedience, the founder's vision of life in community quietly transformed the Western world during a time marked by widespread instability, lawlessness, and poverty.

In addition, Benedict defined spiritual life as a community sharing life together under the guidance of the *Rule*. Benedict's guidebook centers upon Christ, and upon Scripture. Composed in seventy-three short chapters, Benedict's *Rule* is supported by over two hundred quotations from the Bible as well as nearly four hundred scriptural allusions. The *Rule* stands as one of the great evangelical documents of church history. Under the guidance of Christ and the Scriptures, Benedict sought to build a new kind of community based upon life supported by vows, life together under a communal *Rule*, and life under wise leadership.

From these humble beginnings in the early sixth century, Benedict's influence reached across the world through his guidebook and through the thousands of communities seeking to live according to his spiritual vision. Quietly, without much fanfare or recognition, Benedict's legacy transformed the world for Christ.

Is this still possible in our day? Christ continues to empower us today, filling our lives with faith, hope, and love. Christ still sends his followers into this hungry and needy world to transform lives with the gospel through the love of Jesus Christ.

TAKING STEPS
INTO CHRISTIAN FORMATION
from Chapter One

- If you've never read *The Rule of St. Benedict*, pick up a copy and take time to read through this ancient guidebook for yourself. I would recommend reading the *Rule* in an edition that includes a running commentary for nonmonastics, such as Joan Chittister's *The Rule of Benedict: Insights for the Ages* (New York: Crossroad Publishing, 1995).

- Read a biography of one of the great people of faith from church history. Consider some of the lives mentioned in this chapter, such as Benedict, Gregory, Hildegard, or Bernard.

- How do you currently measure spiritual growth in your life or among the people in your family of faith? What "yardsticks" have you found helpful for evaluating progress in the way of life and faith in Christ? Name three ways of measuring how faith, hope, and love are growing in a community of believers.

- Consider opening your local church building to one of the following new ministries, community groups, or local programs: artist guilds, art classes, music instruction, literacy programs, early reader tutorials, SMART reading program, health-care support ministries, parish nursing, elder-senior support programs, a food pantry, a small cottage industry to help the poor in your community, a community garden, children's Bible classes such as Awana ministries. In the past sixteen years, almost all of these outreaches have begun in our community, many of them by the people of Community Presbyterian Church, some of them within the church building.

CHAPTER 2

Benedictine Essentials for the Journey

V eteran backpackers know the ten survival essentials and would never think of hiking without them. They are called *essentials* for a very good reason: they are necessary for survival. According to the Mountaineers, a nonprofit hiking group based in Seattle, Washington, the ten essential items you need when backpacking are: a map, compass, water filter, extra food, raingear, waterproof matches, first aid kit, flashlight with extra bulbs, sunscreen, and sunglasses (see www .mountaineers.org). Slight variations of these ten may be found in various backpacking manuals, but the bottom line is always the same: survival in the wilderness. When faced with life-threatening situations in the great outdoors, hikers rely upon these items to stay alive until help arrives.

What are the survival essentials for the Christian journey? Like opening a hiker's backpack, Benedict's *Rule* begins with spiritual essentials for growing together as a community in Christ. These include spiritual leadership, shared wisdom, tools for spiritual formation, obedience, and humility.

SPIRITUAL LEADERSHIP

The first essential in the Benedictine backpack is spiritual leadership. Benedict places this essential tool at the top of his list, with details for leadership found in several chapters in the *Rule*, including chapter two. Why is spiritual leadership so important? Without it, members of a local congregation lack the guidance, vision, and wisdom needed for growing in their life together in Christ. Think of leadership in terms of outdoor adventures; very few people hike alone on the backcountry trails of our national parks. Most people who backpack in the high country travel in groups of two, three, or four. Often, one lead person in a group has planned the trip, organized the supplies, is more knowledgeable than the others about the trail, and acts informally as a trail guide. When hiking in wilderness high country, several days from the nearest parking lot, people learn to rely upon the wisdom, goodwill, and support of fellow hikers, especially the leader or guide of the adventure. The same holds true with our journey with Christ. We need wise leadership to guide us along the journey of faith in Christ.

Benedict considered leadership a traveling essential for a life of faith. A spiritual leader or mentor represents Christ, and offers guidance along the way. Throughout the *Rule*, leaders are called shepherds (Latin: *pastor*). The Christian model for shepherding is derived from Jesus, who identified himself as the Good Shepherd, the one who calls his sheep by name, leads them out to pasture, cares for them personally, and ultimately, "lays down his life for the sheep" (Jn. 10:11). In his life, death, and resurrection, Jesus fulfills all of the promises of Psalm 23 as shepherd of his sheep. We will explore this theme in greater detail in chapter four.

In our world today, many people prefer to live without any form of leadership, and thus live like sheep without a shepherd. We might liken this to crossing the ocean. There are those rugged individualists who have braved the forces of wind and wave and sailed solo across the ocean. But most people who cross the Atlantic or the Pacific have no problem relying upon wise leaders such as pilots, flight attendants, and air traffic controllers.

Yet, when it comes to the spiritual life, many prefer to journey alone. The act of finding a guide or mentor for one's spiritual life can seem like a countercultural choice in today's world. The image of the individual, standing alone and without need of others, saturates contemporary culture and even seeps into the life of the local church. I too have spent much of my adult life as a believer in Christ without a wise mentor or director. The motives for this avoidance include self-sufficiency, fear of accountability, self-reliance, and laziness. When such a mentor has come into my life, I've often wondered why I had avoided the gift of mentorship, since mentors bring such support, growth, and encouragement. Yet, I understand the self-reliant attitude found among many people in local congregations today. Too often, I come to worship dressed in my Sunday best, smiling at fellow pilgrims, yet somehow unable to share with them that my week has been difficult or that I've been struggling in my spiritual life. Unless we find a spiritual mentor or join a small group where people truly love us, years may pass in the small talk of church life before we begin to feel secure enough to share some of the pain in our lives. In chapter four we will explore Benedict's detailed plan for spiritual guidance within the family of faith—one of the essentials for Christian formation.

SHARED WISDOM

A second essential for the journey of faith is sharing wisdom in community. Many obstacles get in the way of sharing our lives with others in the family of faith, including busy schedules, home commitments, fear of rejection, and time constraints. Yet, according to the Scriptures, God has designed us to live with one another, and spiritual growth flourishes when we enter life together in community.

Consider the wise people who have most influenced your life; those who have invested wisdom, time, and love in your life. Person to person, such shared wisdom can change the world. Benedict considered the sharing of wisdom in community one of the essentials for our journey.

> As often as anything important is to be done in the monastery, the abbot shall call the whole community together and himself explain what the business is. . . . The reason why we have said all should be called for counsel is that the Lord often reveals what is better to the younger. (RB, 3.1, 3)

Two principles emerge from this instruction. First, there is the call to meet together regularly. To ignore the call to meet regularly with others is to ignore the gift of shared wisdom, preferring isolation over involvement with another's life. The challenges of life in community melt away when people begin to truly love one another and learn from each another. Meeting together regularly to share life is no easy task. Yet, God has made humans to live together, in families, in neighborhoods, in groups. All over the world the same pattern exists: people meet to share wisdom and to work out their problems face-to-face. The New Testament warns us against neglecting this pattern. "Let us not give up meeting together, as some are in the habit of doing, but let us encourage one another—and all the more as you see the Day approaching" (Heb. 10:25).

Second, we are wise to include in our communities those who are different from ourselves. The human tendency is to handpick all the members of our inner club, making sure they share our same view-point and outlook on life. Granted, it is easier this way, but Benedict invites us out of the self-made club into real community by saying "all should be called for counsel" (RB, 3.3). We do not just invite the people we like or the people with whom we agree. "All" includes people we would normally overlook, including children. Why invite "all" into decision making? The *Rule* offers a profound reason: "The Lord often reveals what is better to the younger" (RB, 3.3). One of the wise purposes of our meeting with others is to receive the Lord's good counsel. According to the *Rule*, the revelation of wisdom often comes from younger members of a community, such as children, teenagers, young adults, or recent converts. "The younger" may also include recovering addicts, the uneducated, or the poor.

What do such people have to offer adult veterans of the faith? They may offer wisdom from God. The faith community is called together to share wisdom. A spiritual leader is called to actively listen to what is spoken in order to discern the voice of God in the midst of the community, and the people "follow what he judges the wiser course" (RB, 3.2). Shared wisdom often comes from unexpected sources. In his commentary on the *Rule*, Benedictine scholar Terrance Kardong calls chapter three "a surprising chapter." He notes that Benedict makes a significant change in his approach to the monastic life in this chapter by his insistence upon listening to the whole community, especially the counsel of the youngest. Although hierarchical approaches to authority are found throughout the *Rule*, Benedict has no problem setting aside the hierarchy for the sake of growth in Christ. In the hierarchical model, wisdom flows in one direction, from older to younger. Benedict revolutionized Christian formation with his Christlike insistence upon allowing wisdom to flow in both directions, including listening to the young in the community (see Mk. 10:13–16). The Lord's revelation may come to us from those who are younger.

In our local church today, how willing are we to humble ourselves and truly listen to those who are younger and less advanced in the way of Christ? While the hierarchical model continues as the support structure in many church communities around the world today, Benedict's egalitarian approach to sharing wisdom in community offers a fresh way for growth together within the Christian community.

TOOLS FOR SPIRITUAL FORMATION

Like a Swiss Army knife, Benedictine spirituality employs a variety of tools for spiritual formation contained within a single enclosure. Formation is not one single activity but a multifaceted work involving many types of spiritual tools. This is out of necessity, because people are complex creatures. Benedict understood our life of formation as a "workshop where we are to toil faithfully at all these tasks" (RB, 4.78). What tasks? He identified a list of seventy-three "tools of the spiritual craft" (RB, 4.75). A third of these tools for good works listed by Benedict are direct quotations from Scripture that present biblical practices for crafting our life together.

Christian formation is more than concepts and creeds. What is required is a lifelong transformation at the hands of the Master Artist through the use of specific tools of the Spirit. The phrase Benedict uses, *instrumenta artis spiritalis*, literally means "instruments of spiritual arts." He viewed the faith community as God's workshop or art studio—a place where God's artwork in our soul takes place. The result of this loving craftsmanship is beyond our imagining, as Benedict quotes St. Paul: "*What the eye has not seen nor the ear heard, God has prepared for those who love him* (1 Cor. 2:9)" (RB, 4.77).

Within the monastic community, weekly meetings are held to discuss ways of improving the art of communal living in Christ. In the same manner, followers of Christ may find it helpful to discuss Benedict's list of spiritual tools for spiritual formation, and how they might apply within the community of faith. These tools fall into a variety of categories:

RELATIONSHIP WITH GOD. Benedict, echoing Jesus, calls us to love God without reservation, with all our heart, soul, mind, and strength. Such tools that deepen our love for God stand at the top of the list as the chief of all the tools.

RELATIONSHIP WITH BELIEVERS. Benedict lists a variety of tools to build up the body of Christ, such as the second great commandment, "love one another," and complimentary expressions that include "respect one another" and "encourage one another."

CHRISTIAN FORMATION. In his list of tools, Benedict also focuses upon character formation within the individual. This includes shaping such character traits as purity, truth, humility, and holiness. In essence, he calls us to become Christlike in our interior and exterior lives.

SPIRITUAL HABITS. In order for such character to be formed within our lives, we need to develop new habits, also known as spiritual disciplines. Benedict lists such classic disciplines as fasting, prayer, listening to God, watchfulness, and mutual submission.

SERVICE TO OTHERS. Benedict offers a vision for spiritual growth intended to transform the world around us through compassionate service. He includes such practices as helping the poor, caring for the sick, comforting the grieving, making peace, and loving enemies.

As faith pilgrims, when we enter God's art studio, we put our lives into the hands of the Master Artist and allow Christ to form us as he chooses. Allowing God to employ such instruments of the spiritual arts in our lives as described in the *Rule* will not always feel good or be understood by others. Yet, in so doing, we will see our lives gradually shaped into God's beautiful artwork of love, and we will increase our capacity to love others in the workshop of the Lord. See chapter twelve for more on the practical use of tools for spiritual formation.

OBEDIENCE

I did not understand the essence of obedience until I spent an afternoon on the Ocoee River in Tennessee. As I was to lead a group of college students on a white-water rafting adventure, I hired an expert to guide us. He was from a company that had the unique track record of being the only outfitter on the river that had not had a person die in its twenty-five years of rafting adventures. At first I downplayed the pep talk he gave as we geared up, thinking how unnecessary all the warnings were. We are adults after all, not children. Who's going to die from a few hours rafting down a river? As we launched into the Ocoee, the guide warned us, "Follow my commands! If you don't, we'll pay for it." He explained to us that just the week before, someone drowned in that first set of rapids called "Snow White and the Seven Dwarves," "She's not a nice lady!" he shouted over the roaring of the white water, "so follow my commands." We did as he told us, following his commands to paddle forward, paddle backward, or drift. As we submitted to the gift of obedience, we had a blast rafting down the nine miles of white water. Through following commands, we all survived, and had a grand adventure together.

The fourth essential for Christian formation in the *Rule*, "unhesitating obedience," presents a virtue that comes naturally to those who "cherish Christ above all" (RB, 5.1–2). For some today, obedience is not held in high esteem. Rather than seeing obedience as a liberating path to fullness of life and joy, some view this virtue as a straitjacket or an oppressive and unnecessary limitation placed upon personal freedom. My attitude while gearing up for the Ocoee revealed some of this misconception. Why would we want to limit ourselves by placing our will under the authority of another? Yet, when put into contemporary situations, people willingly step into many arenas of obedience without giving it a second thought. For example, anyone who has ever gotten married, played team sports, volunteered for a community service organization, worked for a corporation, or served in the military has become familiar with the value of laying down one's will for the good of others.

One of the spiritual essentials for Christian formation, according to Benedict, is to walk in obedience to God through our accountability to others. Pilgrims who have yielded their hearts to Christ along life's journey learn the joy of laying down their wills in order to listen to God's life-giving commands. As we run our course in the Christian life, like rafting with a river guide through white water, we need guidance to navigate the rapids. Christ gave his followers a few commands to obey such as loving God and loving others. We are formed into the likeness of Christ as we discover the joy of living by obedience to God, putting the instructions of Christ into action in our lives.

We are not traveling alone. The other people in our "raft" are relying upon our willingness to listen and follow the commands of Christ, our river guide. One of the measures of maturity is a willingness to "put aside their own concerns" and "abandon their own will," as "with the ready step of obedience, they follow the voice of authority in their actions" (RB, 5.7–8). When we hear Benedict's call to abandon our wills, we may consider situations in our lives in which the good of others is as important as our own good. We willingly surrender our personal freedom for the sake of our spouse, team, community, company, or country. In our steps, we "follow the voice of authority" in what we choose.

Here again, Benedict employs one of his favorite metaphors of the Christian life, the image of a journey on foot along a pathway. "With the ready step of obedience, they follow the voice of authority in their actions . . . eager to take the narrow road" (RB, 5.8, 11). Spirituality consists of many small daily steps of obedience that add up to a lifelong journey.

When we yield our hearts to the joy of obedience, whether to a coach, commanding officer, boss, spouse, or the needy in our community, we do so out of our love for Christ and our love for one another. "It is love that impels them to pursue everlasting life; therefore, they are eager to take the narrow road of which the Lord says: *Narrow is the road that leads to life* (Matt. 7:14)" (RB, 5.10–11). We obey because we love. We willingly yield our will to God, because we have discovered the delight of "cherish[ing] Christ above all" (RB, 5.2).

There are times when we go through the motions of obedience without yielding our hearts or fully investing our love. The *Rule* warns against heartless, unwilling obedience. Signs of this mock obedience include begrudging or sluggish compliance, halfhearted obedience, and faith actions mixed with grumbling and complaints. Whether done as a means to gain human approval, as a way to assert passive aggression, or as an expression of duplicity of heart, such mock

obedience falls short of God's way along the path of obedience. As
Benedict affirms, "Obedience must be given gladly, for *God loves a
cheerful giver* (2 Cor. 9:7)" (RB, 5.16). Christ, our guide, is looking
for adventurous travelers. Christian formation happens best when
people yield their hearts with joyful surrender to Christ. One of the
great places for launching into the white water of obedience is the
local church, where a joyful heart of submission to God is developed
through humbly offering our lives in obedience to leaders of the
family of faith. When we learn to obey Christ by serving and building up others within the local church, we will discover the delight of
following his commands through the white water of daily life.

TWELVE STEPS OF HUMILITY

The *Big Book* of Alcoholics Anonymous has been the guidebook for
millions of recovering addicts who walk together along the road of
recovery. Alcoholics Anonymous (AA), founded by Bill Wilson and
Dr. Bob Smith in 1935, calls alcoholics and other addicts out of a
destructive way of life into a life of recovery. The miracle of recovery from addiction emerges along the path of twelve steps. Fourteen
hundred years before the creation of AA's path for recovery, another
twelve-step path for recovery was already in place. Instead of recovery
from substance addiction, this earlier twelve-step path involved recovery
from self-centeredness and pride.

In the early sixth century, Benedict created a twelve-step recovery
program that called people to walk these steps in their daily lives—
leading them out of a life centered upon self. C.S. Lewis, in *Mere
Christianity*, wrote,

According to Christian teachers, the essential vice, the utmost evil, is Pride. Unchastity, anger, greed, drunkenness, and all that, are mere fleabites in comparison: it was through Pride that the devil became the devil: Pride leads to every other vice: it is the complete anti-God state of mind.

If the number one trouble in the spiritual life is self-centeredness or pride, the road to recovery is found by walking, step-by-step, into a life of God-centeredness or humility. Benedict's twelve-step program is found in chapter seven of his *Rule*, which opens with these words:

> *Whoever exalts himself shall be humbled, and whoever humbles himself shall be exalted* (Luke 14:11; 18:14). Accordingly, brothers, if we want to reach the highest summit of humility, if we desire to attain speedily that exaltation in heaven to which we climb by the humility in this present life, then by our ascending actions we must set up that ladder. (RB, 7.1, 5–6)

The ladder Benedict sets up is constructed in the human soul, with twelve rungs or steps of humility as the means of our heavenly ascent. Built into this image of the ladder are several creative tensions: body and soul, heaven and earth, divinity and humanity, ascent and descent. Growing in maturity is a divine gift, yet it also requires human effort. At the heart of this holy work is the virtue of humility. It is not optional. If we truly want to be formed into Christlikeness, we will find ourselves climbing this ladder.

RUNG ONE: Put God first. Like the first step in Alcoholics Anonymous that asks for an admission of powerlessness,

Benedict's first step of humility asks us to turn away from self and turn instead to God. "The first step of humility, then, is that a man keeps the *fear of God always before his eyes* (Ps. 36:2) and never forgets it" (RB, 7.10). The invitation is to get our eyes off ourselves and onto God. Scripture tells us that we are powerless to fix our own lives. We will go nowhere in our pilgrim journey until we admit we are powerless to make our life right with God.

RUNG TWO: Imitate Christ. Christ calls us to live as he lived, to imitate his way of living in our daily life. Peter tells us in his first letter, "To this you were called, because Christ suffered for you, leaving you an example, that you should follow in his steps" (2:21). Following in the steps of Christ includes leaving behind our self-willed life and stepping forward into a God-willed life. Recovering alcoholics take step two by coming to believe "that a Power greater than ourselves could restore us to sanity." The second step of recovery calls us to believe in a power greater than ourselves who can restore us to sanity as we imitate Christ—following in his steps. Consider that Jesus encouraged his followers to become like little children. Kids naturally imitate adults, observing and following what we do and say. This second step is to become childlike and imitate Christ in our daily life.

RUNG THREE: Submit to God. Submission is not a popular word today. We would rather do almost anything than submit our lives into the hands of another. Yet, in Alcoholics Anonymous, the third step is the big step of faith, requiring addicts to make "a decision to turn our will and our lives over to the care of God as we understood Him." As mentioned in the preceding section on obedience, besides AA, there are many other arenas of human experience that ask a person to submit themselves to some "higher power," including marriage, sports, careers, and the military. According to Benedict, "A man submits to his superior in all obedience for the love of God, imitating the Lord" (RB, 7.34).

See how one step of humility follows upon the previous? When we begin to imitate Christ, we become interested in living a life of submission, even as Jesus submitted his will to God and "became obedient to death" (Phil. 2:8b). The Greek word for submission, *hupotasso*, calls us to place ourselves under (*hupo*) the ordering (*tasso*) of another. In other words, put God first and live under God's orders. We learn humility by imitating Christ and following the instructions of wise people in our lives. Inherent in this submission is loving accountability—the willingness of two people to check in with one another regularly, ask hard questions, and encourage each other to yield their lives to the grace of God.

RUNG FOUR: Patiently endure. The *Rule* also calls monks to patiently endure hardships within the community. Life is filled with "difficult, unfavorable, or even unjust conditions" (RB, 7.35). In the face of such difficulties, a person on the path of humility does not seek to avoid hardships or to complain against them. Rather, such life challenges are accepted as potential tools used by God to form us. Admittedly, there lies a danger of masochism in all this. We are not asked by God to put up with physical or sexual abuse in a relationship. Yet, there is also the equal and opposite danger of thinking we will never suffer any hardships in our life, as though the

Christian path is strewn with rose petals. We know otherwise. Benedict describes a follower of Christ as one who "quietly embraces suffering and endures it without weakening or seeking escape" (RB, 7.35–36).

In AA's fourth step, addicts make "a searching and fearless moral inventory of [them]selves." As we examine our inner lives, we discover the many ways and times we have hurt or harmed others with our words and deeds. More than mere passivity, patient endurance calls us to reach out to others with goodwill, to bless those who persecute us, to truly love our enemies (see Rom. 12:14).

Corrie Ten Boom suffered greatly at the hands of Nazi soldiers in a concentration camp during World War II. After the war was over, one of her tormentors, a camp guard, came to her to ask for forgiveness. In her book *Tramp for the Lord*, she relates how she was reluctant to forgive this man, but then found herself reaching out her hand to him. "For a long moment we grasped each other's hands, the former guard and the former prisoner. I had never known God's love so intensely as I did then." In this fourth step we are called to actively offer God's forgiveness and grace to all, regardless of how people have treated us—even when we are powerless to do so on our own.

RUNG FIVE: Confess. "The fifth step of humility is that a man does not conceal any sinful thoughts entering his heart, or any wrongs committed in secret, but rather confesses them humbly" (RB, 7.44). To many, this may sound like unwelcome, archaic spirituality. Part of Benedict's world-changing brilliance comes from his willingness to bring the light of Christ into dark corners of human experience. Confession is not easy. I find the act of confession one of the most difficult of all the spiritual disciplines, requiring inner courage and confidence in the mercy of God. However, when I have confessed my sins and have been absolved and restored, I've known the liberating joy of forgiveness, both in my own life and in the lives of many who have come to me to humbly confess their sins. There is a great danger in hiding our evil thoughts and sins committed in secret. We carry heavy burdens of remorse, shame, and guilt from unconfessed sins of the heart. With wisdom, AA challenges addicts in the fifth step: admit to God, to ourselves, and to another human being the exact nature of our wrongs. When I confess my sins, God is faithful and just, and will not only forgive me of my sins, but also cleanse my soul from all unrighteousness (see 1 Jn. 1:9). When we confess to another person, we have an ally—someone who not only bears our burdens with us, but also rejoices with us when we discover the joy of being renewed by God's forgiveness.

RUNG SIX: Learn contentment. "The sixth step of humility is that a monk is content with the lowest and most menial treatment" (RB, 7.49). A Desert Father tells about a man who flew into a rage every time someone insulted him. He went to his mentor to seek help for this problem. The mentor commanded the man for the period of three years to give money to everyone who insulted him. The man went away and did as he was instructed. After the trial period was up, the leader sent the man on a journey to another city. As the man entered the city, someone hurled an insult at him, for which he broke out in laughter. When asked why he was laughing, the man answered, "Because, for three years I have been paying for this kind of thing and now you give it to me for nothing." At this, the man was handed the keys to the city. Habits will not change overnight.

We need God's grace and the gift of time. According to AA, the sixth step is the complete readiness "to have God remove all these defects of character." Over a period of time, we can grow into new ways of living, learning the strange way of living in contentment. We can learn to live simply, like Paul, who "learned the secret of being content in any and every situation, whether well fed or hungry, whether living in plenty of in want" (Phil. 4:12). As we step into the life of humility, we discover the Christlike way of allowing personal attacks and insults to fall upon our lives like rain upon the backs of seabirds.

RUNG SEVEN: Wash feet. One of Jesus' most radical acts took place on the night before he was executed, when he took up a towel and a basin of water and washed the feet of his followers. Such an action was not expected, even by the lowest household servant. A servant was to provide guests with a towel and water. People were expected to wash their own feet. Yet, Jesus willingly stooped low to wash the feet of his followers, and had the audacity to ask us to do the same. As we follow Jesus, we may well ask ourselves, "How low am I willing to go?" Benedict writes these strange words as the seventh step of humility: "A man not only admits with his tongue but is also convinced in his heart that he is inferior to all and of less value" (RB, 7.51). Finding ways to stoop low to "wash feet" is not easy in a culture enamored with power, prestige, and position. In the seventh step of AA, we are challenged to "humbly ask God to remove our shortcomings." The call of Christ to spiritual formation is a countercultural invitation into a whole new way of living—a servant-hearted, radical lifestyle marked by asking God for help in washing our lives clean, and then offering that same gift to others by serving people in their places of greatest need.

RUNG EIGHT: Be accountable. "The eighth step of humility is that a monk does only what is endorsed by the common rule of the monastery and by the example set by his superiors" (RB, 7.55). News stories arise every year about ethical and financial disasters wrought in the corporate world due to the lack of accountability. Yet, few people enjoy having people snoop over their shoulders to check up on their work. Most of us do not like being held accountable for our actions. People seeking recovery from addictive lifestyles know their need for accountability to others. The eighth step of AA requires addicts "to make a list of all persons we have harmed, and be willing to make amends to them all." Benedict also assumed accountability as one of the necessary practices for Christian formation. The eighth step of humility holds us accountable to Christ, to Scripture, and to wise spiritual mentors, such as pastors, priests, teachers, and other mature leaders, whose example we can follow as we mature in the Lord.

RUNG NINE: Learn to listen. The first word in the Rule is "listen" (Latin: *obsculta*). This is no accidental beginning. Benedict spent his first several years as a monk alone in the cave of Subiaco. He was learning to pray by listening. Prayer is a two-way relationship. In our relationship with

God, consider who has more to say. Benedict calls monks to silence in the monastery so that with their ears and their hearts they will learn to listen. At the end of his famous "Sermon on the Mount," Jesus declared, "Therefore everyone who hears these words of mine and puts them into practice is like a wise man" (Matt. 7:24). Obedience to God requires that we listen with the "ear of [our] heart," and faithfully put into action what we have heard (RB, prologue 1). When we give our tongues free rein, we are unable to listen. Scripture is full of warnings against the misuse of words. The ninth step of AA not only encourages people to make verbal amends, but it also warns against the thoughtless use of words. "We make direct amends to such people wherever possible, except when to do so would injure them or others." When our words have the potential of harming others, we are wise to restrain our speech. James writes, "Likewise the tongue is a small part of the body, but it makes great boasts. Consider what a great forest is set on fire by a small spark. The tongue also is a fire, a world of evil among the parts of the body" (Jas. 3:5–6a). The ninth step of humility instructs us to listen by keeping our tongue in check. God is speaking through Scripture and through people around us. We are invited to learn to listen.

RUNG TEN: Laugh. The further up the ladder of humility a person climbs, the more reason we have for laughter and joy. Why is this so? The closer we come to Christ, the less we have to lose. The steps of humility are a gradual stripping away of our self-centered way of living. In the tenth step of AA, we are asked to continually evaluate our progress along the way to recovery. "We continue to take personal inventory and when we are wrong, we promptly admit it." As we continue to die to self and live for God, our hearts will indeed begin to "overflow with the inexpressible delight of love," just as Benedict promised (RB, prologue 49). I've often witnessed this overflow of delight at a Benedictine monastery in the form of laughter. Why then does the *Rule* warn followers of Christ against laughter? "The tenth step of humility is that he is not given to ready laughter" (RB, 7.9). Laughter, like colors, come in many shades. Creative, joyful laughter radiates like new shoots in a springtime garden. Destructive or spiteful laughter sickens the soul like bile or vomit. C.S. Lewis, in *The Screwtape Letters*, writes of four forms of laughter: "I divide the causes of human laughter into Joy, Fun, the Joke Proper, and Flippancy." This last form of humor not only tears down what God has built up, but it also hardens the very soil within the human soul where growth might have taken place. As Lewis puts it, "Flippancy builds up around a man the finest armour-plating. . . . It deadens instead of sharpening, the intellect." Such laughter dishonors God and God's creative work within the human soul. On the other hand, joy, fun, and play build up the soul, allowing us to take ourselves less seriously, and to learn to take delight in God's unfolding new creation.

RUNG ELEVEN: Practice gentleness. When hikers backpack in the national parks, they practice "leave no trace" hiking. Our goal is to walk gently upon the land. The way of humility is to walk gently upon the land, and to speak with gentleness toward others. "The eleventh step of humility is that a monk speaks gently . . . with becoming modesty, briefly and reasonably, but without raising his voice, as it is written: 'A wise man is known by his few words'" (RB, 7.60–61). The virtue of gentleness is easily overlooked in a culture caught up with power and position. When we focus on our own needs and desires, we are often inattentive to the needs of others. Gentleness calls us to step beyond these barriers into a life of consideration toward others. Benedictine formation challenges us to consider the hurts and the vulnerable places in the lives of people around us. We all need help to live such a life. AA, in the eleventh step, reminds recovering people to pray and meditate—to draw upon God's help: "We seek through prayer and meditation to improve our conscious contact with God, as we understood Him, praying only for knowledge of His will for us and the power to carry that out." Humility calls us to stand gently upon the earth, to step into the shoes of another, to leave only the trace of Christ's love.

RUNG TWELVE: Live a life of humility. Where is this ladder of humility leading us? What if all of this emphasis on humility changes me into a doormat upon which the world wipes its shoes? The marvel of humility is that just the opposite happens. The further up the ladder we climb and the more we die to our self-centered way of living, the more we gain confidence to live fully as the person God made us to be, giving us an even greater capacity to truly engage hurting people in this world with Christ's love. Many people have a "Tupperware" understanding of the spiritual life. In this view, faith and religion are kept in plastic containers with sealed lids. Our faith seldom mixes with the rest of our lives. Such people tend to ignore God at their workplace, in a restaurant, or while making love, or knitting a scarf. Those realms are in their own separate plastic containers called Career, Food, Sex, and Hobbies. Religion is just one more container. Benedict saw the Christian life differently. Spirituality is more like the coolant in the refrigerator. It infuses every container, moving right through the plastic lids and containers, keeping everything fresh and new. The ladder of humility moves us away from a compartmentalized approach to God. We begin to allow God into every aspect of our life, infusing our life with freshness. Like the twelfth step of AA that calls us to live the principles of AA in all our affairs, Benedict closes his twelve steps with a call to live a lifestyle of humility: "The twelfth step of humility is that a monk always manifests humility in his bearing no less than in his heart, so that it is evident at the Work of God, in the oratory, the monastery or the garden, on a journey or in the field, or anywhere else" (RB, 7.62–63). Benedict understood humility to be a lifelong journey: "If we want to reach the highest summit of humility, if we desire to attain speedily that exaltation in heaven to which we climb by the humility of this present life, then by our ascending actions we must set up that ladder" (RB, 7.5–6).

TAKING STEPS
INTO CHRISTIAN FORMATION
from Chapter Two

- Go for a day hike into God's creation to reflect upon spiritual essentials for the journey of Christian formation.

- If you don't currently have a spiritual mentor, consider finding one—then meet together at least monthly.

- Consider the wise people who have most influenced your life and faith. Write down how these people invested their lives in your personal spiritual growth in Christ. What have you learned from them?

- If you do not currently meet regularly with a small group of fellow pilgrims, consider joining such a group within your local church, or forming a new group. Call together six to eight people and share with them your desire to meet regularly. Talk together about the design of the group, how often you'll meet, what you'll study, and who will be the facilitator. Then begin meeting together for spiritual growth.

- Put into practice the "tools for spiritual formation," following ideas listed at the end of chapter twelve.

- Read through the "twelve steps of humility" again. Pick out one or two of these steps that seem most challenging to you at this time. Seek God's help in stepping out by faith and putting that step into practice in your life this month.

CHAPTER 3

The Path of Communal Prayer

Everyone knows the difference between a trail map and a trail. The former offers a picture of the way, including such important details as landmarks, distances, and topography. Wise hikers study trail maps prior to arriving at the trailhead in order to gain information regarding the challenges on the journey ahead. But once along the trail, the map is tucked away in a backpack for future reference. The practical business of hiking takes precedence over the preparatory business of studying maps.

In similar fashion, the Christian life involves studying maps as well as hiking upon paths. Following Christ requires becoming a "traveler," not merely a "balconeer" who watches others. When Christ calls us to follow him, he invites us to set out upon a life-long journey, traveling into our new life with God and with others. Christ's first followers asked him, "Lord, teach us to pray" (Lk. 11:1). We are all amateurs at prayer. We pray because we love. In Latin, love (*ama*) is the root of the word *amateur*, reminding us that amateurs do what they do out of love, not because they have a degree or are being paid. In his prologue, Benedict declares, "We intend to establish a school for the Lord's service," anticipating all who enter this school to become lifelong learners of prayer. One-fifth of the chapters of the *Rule* provide guidance in a life of communal prayer. Just as the unseen air we breathe surrounds our lives, so the unseen presence of God surrounds us, always ready to inspire us and enliven us throughout the day and night. I would like to explore ancient patterns of prayer with you in this chapter, and to discover how these time-tested approaches to prayer may deepen our life together in Christ.

PRAYING IN THE DARK

Most people learn to pray at night. If you learned to pray as a child, it was likely at bedtime. Children are often afraid of the dark and cry out for help in the night. Learning to pray in the dark can bring us right back to our childhood, which is a good thing. Jesus calls us to become like little children in order to enter the kingdom of God. Even adults are afraid of dark forces that threaten to undo us. So we pray in the dark. We cry out to the unseen God in the dark times of our lives—calling for help in the night.

Jonah may be considered the patron saint of those who pray in the dark. He cried out to the Lord from the darkness of the belly of the fish. "From inside the fish Jonah prayed to the LORD his God. He said: 'In my distress I called to the LORD, and he answered me. From the depths of the grave I called for help, and you listened to my cry'" (Jonah 2:1–2). Jonah's prayer consisted of an odd assortment of quotations from the Hebrew Scriptures, mostly from the Psalms. In his darkest hour, Jonah prayed the memorized prayers from his childhood, drawn from the prayer book of the Bible—the Psalms.

Benedict took up this practice of praying in the dark, calling his monks to wake up in the middle of the night to pray the Psalms together in the dark "belly" of the sanctuary. The *Rule* offers insights for praying in the dark. "During the winter season, that is, from the first of November until Easter, it seems reasonable to arise at the eighth hour of the night" (RB, 8.1).

Besides sleep, very few activities "seem reasonable" to me at two in the morning. Yet, I've spoken to many people who find themselves awake at that time, unable to get back to sleep. We can learn to pray in those dark hours, calling out on the name of the Lord, using the words of Scripture as our cry in the night. Benedict encourages his monks to pray the Psalms during the early morning hours before dawn, both together and in solitude. His monks spent a few hours each morning before dawn reciting psalms. The word he uses for study, *meditationi*, refers to vocal recitation of a text until it is memorized.

A practical note for those who are learning to pray in the dark: there is great wisdom in memorizing some of the Psalms. This discipline instructs our hearts to call out to God in the night without disturbing others. You may begin your practice by learning the nightly prayer time known as Vigils. This office includes singing the Psalms and reciting Scripture lessons, if possible from memory. These two nightly spiritual disciplines are available to nonmonks by opening the Scriptures and reading aloud the text of a psalm along with a passage from one of the Gospels or New Testament letters, as we offer our heart to God in prayer. "I will praise the LORD, who counsels me; even at night my heart instructs me" (Ps. 16:7).

One of the loveliest insights from Scripture on praying in the dark comes from Paul's letter to the Romans, where he teaches that God knows the weaknesses and the difficulties we face in prayer. "In the same way, the Spirit helps us in our weakness. We do not know what we ought to pray for, but the Spirit himself intercedes for us with groans that words cannot express. . . . The Spirit intercedes for the saints in accordance with God's will" (Rom. 8:26–27).

MORNING PRAYER

In the Gospel of Mark, we discover Jesus' practice of morning prayer. "Very early in the morning, while it was still dark, Jesus got up, left the house and went off to a solitary place, where he prayed" (Mk. 1:35). On the previous day, after teaching and healing in the local synagogue on the Sabbath, Jesus retired to Simon Peter's home in Capernaum. After sunset, Mark tells us, "the people brought to Jesus all the sick and demon-possessed. The whole town gathered at the door, and Jesus healed many who had various diseases" (1:32–34). Late that night, Jesus was finally able to get some much-needed sleep. Though Jesus was exhausted from intensive ministry to sick and needy people, he still got up before dawn, heeding a deeper call—a call to prayer. By this act, Jesus reveals the importance of intimacy with God in prayer during the early hours of the day. For Jesus, prayer holds a higher priority than much-needed sleep.

Benedict followed Jesus' pattern for morning prayer, calling the monastic community to wake before the dawn, leave the comfort of the bed, and journey into a place of prayer. He called his monks to communal prayer every morning of the year, firmly establishing prayer as the first priority of each new day. Benedictine prayer times for the early morning are clearly laid out in chapters eleven through thirteen of the *Rule*, including details of the number of psalms to be sung, as well as instructions regarding readings, hymns, responses, canticles, and prayers. Some of these acts of Morning Prayer are to be "recited by heart" (see RB, 12.4), revealing again Benedict's commitment to memorization. The practical reason for this memorization is two-fold: we are able to meditate upon Scripture without turning on any lights during the dark hours of the morning; but more importantly, God's Word becomes an internal part of our lives even while we are still sleepy. While Benedict's guidance for Morning Prayer involves many liturgical details, the Morning Prayer services center on praying the Psalms. In the summer season, when the nights are shorter and the Morning Prayer service needs to be shortened to allow for "the monks who happen to arise too late" (see RB, 11.12), Benedict offers a moderate adjustment, recommending a shorter time of Scripture readings, while keeping the same number of psalms.

The *Rule* also places priority on daily recitation of the Lord's Prayer, at the end of Morning Prayer, "for all to hear, because thorns of contention are likely to spring up" (RB, 13.12). Benedict understood the value of reciting the Lord's Prayer for forgiveness, recognizing the likelihood of relational troubles springing up during the day. This preemptive prayerful approach to contention within the community helps weed out troubles before they have opportunity to root themselves in the heart of the community. Most churches today recite aloud the words of the Lord's Prayer every week as part of worship.

Several years ago, our local congregation began singing the Lord's Prayer together on the first Sunday of the month before receiving the sacrament of the Lord's Supper. This single act of worship stands as one of the most moving acts of devotion in our community of faith. The Lord's Prayer unites local voices of believers with the whole body of Christ.

What can we learn from monastic guidance for prayer in the morning hours? We can make the practice of morning prayer a daily routine, as habitual as our practice of morning hygiene. Just as natural as a morning shower or brushing our teeth, we can take time each morning to enjoy prayer with God. Within this practice, we are wise to pray the Psalms, sing songs of faith, and pray the Lord's Prayer. This habit can be practiced in solitude as well as in community. Readers who currently do not pray in the morning may find it helpful to begin by adding a short morning time of prayer into their personal daily lives.

If you already have a set habit of morning prayer, you might try meeting in the morning once or twice a week with a few other Christians for prayer. If such a group currently does not exist in your local church, consider inviting a few others to join you weekly and begin praying together for the church. I've been involved with two such groups for seventeen years, and have found great encouragement and strength through these weekly morning prayer groups. Through the winter season, these gatherings begin in the dark. As the psalmist wrote long ago, "Awake my soul . . . I will awaken the dawn" (Ps. 57:8). To begin the time of morning prayer, pray aloud the words of a psalm, allowing the words to instruct and influence your prayers. Pilgrims are wise to pray together. Benedict chose a variety of morning psalms for the monks to pray each week.

Another addition to our morning times with God might include singing songs and hymns together. A favorite hymnbook or songbook may be set near the place where we awake. Upon arising in the morning, we open our mouths to make a joyful noise to the Lord, offering our heart's song of gratitude for the new day. During Sunday morning worship, offer prayers in song together, joining hearts and voices by singing psalms, hymns, and spiritual songs together as a community of faith. Weekly, as a church family, we lift up our hearts and voices in song as a communal prayer to the Lord.

Dietrich Bonhoeffer declared the importance of morning prayer in the last chapter of his little guide to praying the Psalms:

> The entire day received order and discipline when it acquires unity.
> This unity must be sought and found in morning prayer. It is confirmed

in work. The morning prayer determines the day. Squandered time of which we are ashamed, temptations to which we succumb, weaknesses and lack of courage in work, disorganization and lack of discipline in our thoughts and in our conversation with other men, all have their origin most often in the neglect of morning prayer. Order and distribution of our time become more firm where they originate in prayer. Temptations which accompany the working day will be conquered on the basis of the morning breakthrough to God.

PRAYING THE PSALMS

For thousands of years, the Psalms have stood as the centerpiece of prayer within the community of faith. Today, the Psalms often get neglected, standing like a beautiful building from the distant past that now lies in ruins among the lives of busy people. Today, the Psalms are rarely the central practice of a vital prayer life. Why renovate this ancient practice of praying the Psalms? The Jewish people have always viewed the book of Psalms as their prayer book, the instruction manual for the life of prayer, both in community and in solitude. Jesus prayed the Psalms from the cross—two of the last seven sentences he prayed from the cross are direct quotations from the Psalms, including Psalm 22:1a (cf. Mk. 15:34) and Psalm 31:5a (cf. Lk. 23:46). Jesus may have been silently praying these two psalms in their entirety from memory while suffering on the cross, only vocalizing the two sentences recorded in the Gospels. Jesus often quoted from the book of Psalms, opening this prayer book of the Bible to show his followers what was spoken long ago concerning his life and purpose (see Lk. 24:44). The early church learned to pray the Psalms in the midst of crisis when calling upon the name of the Lord in community (Acts 4:24–26).

Throughout history, the Psalms have offered security, strength, guidance, and comfort to communities, congregations, families, and countless individuals. From our distant past, like a wise old sage, Benedict calls us to rebuild the ancient practice of praying through the Psalms, reestablishing psalmody as a central stronghold of our life with God. If you attend a worship service at a Benedictine monastery, you will quickly discover that most of the service is antiphonal praying of the Psalms. Antiphonal singing (Greek: *anti*, opposite + *phone*, voice) involves the singing of alternating parts by a choir or congregation divided into two or more sections. Monks stand facing each other across the choir stalls, responsively chanting the Psalms, line by line, verse by verse, throughout the day, every day of the year. No psalm is missed. No day is without the gift of the book of Psalms.

Benedict called faith communities to pray the Psalms throughout the day at set hours known as the Divine Office, or the Work of God (Latin: *Opus Dei*). These hours of communal prayer have also become known as the Liturgy of the Hours. The main prayer work during these Benedictine services is the vocal praying of the Psalms. In Benedict's day, the monastic community prayed every word of all 150 psalms every week together. As he admonished his monks,

> The full complement of one hundred and fifty psalms is by all means carefully maintained every week, and the series begins anew each Sunday at Vigils. For monks who in a week's time say less that the full psalter with the customary canticles betray extreme indolence and lack of devotion in their service. We read, after all, that our holy Fathers, energetic as they were, did all this in a single day. Let us hope that we, lukewarm as we are, can achieve it in a whole week. (RB, 18.23–25)

In the monastery, Compline stands as the last prayer time in the daily Liturgy of the Hours, a service often celebrated at 7:30 in the evening. The *Rule* calls monks to pray the same three psalms every night: Psalms 4, 91, and 134. As a contemporary discipline, this may seem unnecessarily repetitive, but for a monk, the psalms of the night prepare the heart for sleeping in peace. A beautiful spirit of calm descends upon the one who prays these final prayers of the day. For years in our home, we have prayed together one of the nighttime psalms as we say goodnight: "I will lie down and sleep in peace, for you alone, O LORD, make me dwell in safety" (Ps. 4:8). After Compline, the monks enter what is known as the "great silence," broken only by the psalmist's call to Vigils early in the morning to begin the next day of prayer: "O Lord, open my lips, and my mouth will declare your praise" (Ps. 51:15).

While the local church is not a monastery, the distinction between monastery and congregation is not as dramatic as it may seem at first. Both monastery and local church are intentional communities of faith in Christ, with the mutual purpose of gathering regularly for common worship and prayer. The book of Psalms is the prayer book of the Bible, given to the church by God for our edification. One of the keys to building up our life in Christ begins with the practice of praying from Jesus' prayer book, the book of Psalms.

Practically speaking, whether we are alone or part of a group, we might begin learning to pray the Psalms using the Psalms of the Day method. According to this approach, every day five psalms are waiting to instruct us along our journey. The Psalms of the Day include every thirtieth psalm according to the day of the month. On the fifth day of the month we open to Psalm 5, 35, 65, 95, or 125. On the twenty-first day of the month, Psalm 21, 51, 81, 111, or 141. We save the "queen of the

Psalter," Psalm 119, with her 176 verses, for months with thirty-one days. In this manner, we keep stretching our prayer life by stepping beyond our favorites, allowing the whole book of Psalms to be our guide.

DEVELOPING A LIFE OF PRAYER

There is no such thing as instant spiritual growth. Christian formation happens through days and nights, across many seasons and years. How can a person of faith develop a life of prayer? I would like to conclude this chapter on communal prayer by looking at four practical approaches to prayer I've learned from monks.

DEVELOP A DAILY RHYTHM OF PRAYER. First, seek to create set times in your daily schedule for prayer. Benedict called his monks to pray seven times a day, citing Psalm 119:164, *"Seven times a day I have praised you"* (RB, 16.1). Though gathering together with others seven times a day will be prohibitive for most Christians, we are wise to set aside special times throughout the day for personal prayer, including morning, noon, and evening. One of the great helps for growing in this daily rhythm of prayer is the use of a prayer book. Many such prayer books are in print and readily available, including five of my favorites:

- *The Book of Common Prayer*
- *The Glenstal Book of Prayer: A Benedictine Prayer Book*
- *Work of God: Benedictine Prayer*
- *A Guide to Prayer*
- *Celtic Daily Prayer*

All these prayer books feature an outline for prayer to guide you into the presence of the Lord at set times of the day. Of course, one of the main designs uniting all such books is praying the Psalms. Most of these books offer morning and evening prayers, though some add prayer outlines for other times of the day as well. Finding times every day for prayer becomes a joy and delight when we recall the words of the psalmist who sang long ago:

> How priceless is your unfailing love! Both high and low among men find refuge in the shadow of your wings. They feast on the abundance of your house; you give them drink from your river of delights. For with you is the fountain of life; in your light we see light. (Ps. 36:7–9)

Our life of prayer will truly become a feast on the abundance of God's house when we make time for God in our daily lives.

CREATE A PRAYER PLACE. Second, try creating a prayer place in your home. This place can be as simple as a comfortable chair in a certain room. As a practical matter, include a good reading light, a Bible, a prayer book, a journal, and perhaps a music player. Find peaceful instrumental or choral music that helps you enter into the quiet of God's presence. I also like lighting candles in a prayer place. Go to this place in the morning and again in the evening. I'll admit to being sporadic in my prayer habits and have several places in my home where I go for prayer. Yet, I enjoy being in God's presence in a prayer place within our home.

Also, consider developing a place for prayer in your local church building. If your church currently does not have a dedicated prayer room, bring the idea up before the leadership team or pastoral staff and see how the Lord might move the congregation to create such a place. Benedict set aside a place within the community for prayer. "The oratory ought to be what it is called, and nothing else is to be done or stored there" (RB, 52.1). The oratory in a monastery is a place devoted solely to prayer, where brothers or sisters "may simply go in and pray, not in a loud voice, but with tears and heartfelt devotion" (RB, 52.4). Many local congregations have set aside such a place, a prayer room, with a few comfortable chairs, a kneeling bench, a good reading lamp, and a table upon which is placed a Bible and perhaps a few prayer books.

CELEBRATE SEASONS OF PRAYER. Benedict recognized the changing of the seasons as part of the rhythm of a life of prayer. Monks follow the sacred liturgical cycle, including the annual celebration of "feasts of saints, and indeed on all solemn festivals" (RB, 14.1). On these special days, followers of Christ remember the great deeds of God: the birth, life, death, and resurrection of Jesus Christ. The annual church calendar helps center our attention on Jesus Christ through the seasons of the year. Learn to celebrate the holy seasons of Advent, Christmas, Epiphany, Lent, Easter, and Pentecost. Each of these seasons has a special gift to offer us in our journey of faith. Throughout the church year, we are also wise to remember the feast days of the saints, taking time to learn of their lives and to remember their unique gifts and callings. When we hold up the portraits of the great heroes who have journeyed on the path of prayer before us, the saints encourage us along the way of Christian formation. In my reading on the lives of saints, I've often received strength and guidance for the journey ahead by looking back at the remarkable lives from the past.

LEARN TO PRAY THE JESUS PRAYER. In the midst of every season, a life of prayer is something we practice daily, in the morning, through the day, in the evening, and into the night. One of the classic expressions of continuous prayer is found in the Jesus Prayer. In *The Way of the Pilgrim*, the anonymous author describes a pilgrim's dilemma of trying to understand what Paul meant when he wrote, "pray continually" (1 Thess. 5:17). Finally, a monk teaches the pilgrim the secret of unceasing prayer—that is, to pray a simple prayer known as the Jesus Prayer: Lord Jesus Christ (inhale), Son of God (exhale), have mercy on me (inhale), a sinner (exhale). Pray this simple prayer in unison with the pattern of breathing. Those who are new to this way of prayer may think this approach to prayer amounts to vain repetition of words—the very type of prayer Jesus warned us against in the Sermon on the Mount. But soon the Jesus Prayer becomes a regular way of prayer, a gift through the day and night returning our attention again and again to the true center of our lives in Jesus Christ. This form of prayer keeps the name of Jesus nearer to us than words or thoughts and helps us draw our whole being into the presence of our Lord. Some have called it the prayer of the heart.

A life of prayer does not come easily. We learn to pray by training ourselves daily, because many interruptions, distractions, and lesser activities will constantly threaten to crowd prayer out of our lives. Benedict concluded his tour of the village of prayer by reminding us about the heart of prayer, which is nothing less than intimacy with "the Lord God of all things" (see RB, 20.2). We are called into a heart-to-heart relationship with God. This is no ordinary matter. "Let us consider, then, how we ought to behave in the presence of God and his angels" (RB, 19.6). A life of prayer is a life of "the utmost humility and sincere devotion" before God (see RB, 20.2). Our prayers are not heard for their many words, but for "our purity of heart" (see RB, 20.3). As a layperson, Benedict was not interested in prayer as religious words and liturgical formulas. Instead, he viewed a life of prayer as a person's genuine heart devotion before the God of "all things"—a life of intimacy lived daily with God within a community of fellow believers.

TAKING STEPS
INTO CHRISTIAN FORMATION

from Chapter Three

- "Lord, teach us to pray" (Lk. 11:1). Make this your nightly prayer for a month.

- Very early in the morning, while it is still dark, wake up, get up, go to a solitary place, and spend time praying in the dark. How does this time for prayer differ from other times of prayer in your life?

- Consider meeting with others for weekly morning prayer. If such a prayer group does not currently exist in your local church, ask a few others to help you begin a morning prayer group that meets every week at the same time and place.

- Pray through the Psalms according to the Psalms of the Day pattern. Teach this pattern to others and have them join you in learning to pray the Psalms.

- Develop a life of prayer by adding a daily rhythm of prayer to your schedule, creating a prayer place in your home or church, celebrating seasons of prayer through the year, and learning to pray the Jesus Prayer.

CHAPTER 4

The Path of Spiritual Guidance

During my first retreat to a monastery in October 1986, I met with Father Peter, who was serving as Retreat Master at that time. As a young pastor just two years out of seminary, I was weary, anxious, and insecure in my life and faith. As a spiritual director, Father Peter offered me the extraordinary gift of listening. Over twenty years later, that single hour of guidance still stands as one of the definitive turning points in my faith journey. Benedict invites us to explore the art of spiritual guidance. In the following pages, I want to build upon our earlier look at spiritual leadership and discover what the *Rule* has to teach us today about the practice of leadership, pastoral care, admonition, and guidance in community.

LESSONS ON LEADERSHIP

How do people become leaders in a community? Some are elected, some are appointed, and some appoint themselves to govern the people. Still others emerge naturally from within the community and are gradually recognized for their maturity and wisdom, although they have no formal appointment to place them into a position of leadership. Within a community of faith, leaders are called to provide guidance in the faith journey of the people. Such leaders offer guidance through the example of their lives and through their service to the people, emulating Jesus, who declared, "For even the Son of Man did not come to be served, but to serve, and to give his life as a ransom for many" (Mk. 10:45).

Just as within a monastery, the community of a local congregation is governed by a variety of servant-leaders. These servant-leaders may include small group leaders (in the monastery: *deans*), ministry leaders (the *porter* and the *cellarer* are two such positions in a monastery), assistant coleaders (in the monastery: the *prior* or *prioress*), and the main spiritual leader over the whole community (in the monastery: the *abbot* or *abbess*). Benedict drew upon the biblical precedent for leadership structures, incorporating the wisdom of Jethro, Moses' father-in-law, who urged Moses to appoint leaders over groups of one thousand, one hundred, fifty, and ten (Exod. 18:13–26; Deut. 1:9–18). Benedict envisioned small group leaders, or deans (*decani*), in charge of a group of ten monks. All servant-leaders need regular encouragement, guidance, and training by other leaders.

Churches can be distinguished by their unique approaches to leadership. How are leaders chosen? What is the role of leadership within the community? What structures of leadership help a local congregation grow in faith, hope, and love? Some appoint leaders from the top down; some elect leaders from the grassroots. Some leaders serve for life and some serve for limited terms. Each of these structures of leadership has developed within specific historic settings, often as a corrective to some perceived excess within another group, or as an attempt to return to a model of leadership discerned from Scripture. Annually, pastors, elders, and other servant-leaders within local churches face the task of recruiting and training new leaders for the care of the congregation. What lessons in leadership might we learn from the *Rule* to improve our practice of leadership within a faith community today?

ENCOURAGE A MODEL OF SERVANT LEADERSHIP. I've served as pastor in Cannon Beach since 1993. Over the years, we've called our elders and deacons "servant-leaders," emphasizing the role of service and leading by example. This approach to leadership with humility is something I've learned from Benedict, who tells us to choose leaders "for their good repute and holy life . . . for virtuous living and wise teaching" (RB, 21.1, 4). The primary qualifications for servant-leaders are wisdom and maturity in Christ. The *Rule* places many checks and balances upon the hierarchy of power within the monastery. The abbot seeks to serve the people, following the example of Christ, who laid down his life for the sheep. "Rather, he should keep in mind that he has undertaken the care of souls for whom he must give an account" (RB, 2.34). Encourage a spirit of joyful service among the leaders involved in the local church by lifting up the example of Christ washing his disciples' feet the night before he went to the cross.

LEADERS RECRUIT AND TRAIN OTHER LEADERS. A second lesson for leadership within a faith community includes the willingness to delegate leadership to other wise leaders. A leader is asked to "share the burdens of his office" (RB, 21.3). Entrust other leaders to carry out the work of spiritual leadership alongside those already in places of responsibility. One of the biggest hurdles to growth within many local churches is not raising up new leadership. When church leaders, including pastors, refuse to "share the burdens of their office" with other wise leaders within the local church, congregations will suffer. Assistant leaders within the monastery (priors) are warned against becoming "puffed up by the evil spirit of pride and thinking of themselves as second abbots" (RB, 65.2). Lest there be any attempt to "usurp tyrannical power and foster contention and discord in their communities" (RB, 65.2), Benedict places the abbot in charge of the monastery with a variety of other leaders under his care, including priors and deans. "If possible, as we have already established, the whole operation of the monastery should be managed through deans under the abbot's direction. Then, so long as it is entrusted to more than one, no individual will yield to pride" (RB, 65.12–13). Using the terms *dean*, *senior*, and *elder* interchangeably in the *Rule*, Benedict places leaders in charge of groups of junior monks, especially in the dormitories where monks sleep. These seniors, or deans, help younger monks avoid the temptations of the flesh, overseeing them through the watches of the night. In another section of the *Rule*, Benedict refers to elders, saying that they, like the abbot, are to hear the confession of sins from the monks in confidence, "who know how to heal their own wounds as well as those of others, without . . . making them public" (RB, 46.6). The principle here involves recruiting and empowering lay leaders to care for the lives of people. Such lay leaders bring care to such a personal level that people feel secure enough to open their lives in confidence and to find God's gifts of forgiveness and healing for their wounded souls.

APPOINT ELDERS TO SERVE THE PEOPLE OF GOD. In my first year as a pastor in Cannon Beach, the pastor of a neighboring church came to me to ask for guidance in developing the role of elders in that congregation. Up until that time, they had only deacons and now had decided to add the leadership role of elder. Since the Presbyterian Church has been ordaining elders to serve the people of God for five hundred years, I had plenty of resources to offer my pastor friend. The role of elder in a faith community dates back into ancient Jewish history. Among ancient Jewish communities, elders were called to serve as leaders, judges, and caretakers of the people of Israel. In the New Testament, the office of elder within the early church is one of spiritual nurture and oversight within the local community of faith. According to the New Testament, an elder is to be "blameless—not overbearing, not quick-tempered, not given to drunkenness, not violent, not pursuing dishonest gain. Rather he must be hospitable, one who loves what is good, who is self-controlled, upright, holy and disciplined" (Titus 1:7–8). Within the Presbyterian Church, a congregation is governed by a team of elders, chosen by congregational election to serve for a three-year term. At Community Presbyterian Church, we have nine elders, wise laypeople who oversee the care of the congregation. The title *Presbyterian* originates from the Greek word used in the New Testament for "elder," *presbyteros*, or wise lay leaders who govern the community of believers. Within the Presbyterian Church, elders meet regularly for prayer, direction, and shared counsel regarding the care of the church. As a pastor in the Presbyterian Church, I've learned from Benedict to rely upon the wisdom of these elected elders in directing the spiritual care of the people, leading in worship, teaching the Scriptures, visiting the sick, and offering spiritual guidance to the people.

TRAIN LEADERS TO CARE FOR PEOPLE. The primary calling for spiritual leaders is not church business, but the care of people: giving informal spiritual guidance, praying together, and living an exemplary life in Christ. When spiritual leaders begin to understand this, a congregation will grow and flourish in their faith-life together in Christ. Spiritual leadership within the *Rule* is described with such images as parenting, gardening, healing, and shepherding. Within the local church, we are wise to evaluate our understanding of leadership as well as to invest time regularly in nurturing the life of those who offer leadership, implementing Benedict's wise understanding of the care of people.

SHEPHERDING SOULS

Recently, the people of Community Presbyterian Church commissioned an elder to serve as their lay pastor, empowering him to serve the church through the ministry of teaching, preaching, and caring for souls. Those whom the people choose to serve as overseers within the local church are to be people of "goodness of life and wisdom in teaching" (RB, 64.2). One of the most important investments of a pastor for the benefit of the whole church is in the training of leaders in the art of spiritual direction. When our elders and deacons meet together, I've found it a wise practice to nurture these leaders by taking time for group spiritual direction. The goal is simply to build up the servant-leaders within the congregation so that they will be better equipped to shepherd the people. Benedict offers helpful guidance for the development of shepherding within a community of faith. Below, I offer five Benedictine principles for shepherding of souls:

FOLLOW CHRIST'S EXAMPLE. The picture of pastoring care as shepherding is taken from the life of Jesus, our Shepherd. The imagery of shepherding is found throughout Scripture as a metaphor for care of people. As the *Rule* describes this role of guidance as shepherding:

> [We are] to imitate the loving example of the Good Shepherd who left the ninety-nine sheep in the mountains and went in search of the one sheep that has strayed. So great was his compassion for its weakness that *he* mercifully *placed it on his sacred shoulders* and so carried it back to the flock (Luke 15:5). (RB, 27.8–9)

The first principle for shepherding is that we follow the example of our loving Shepherd, seeking out the lost, bringing them back into the fold of God's grace within the community. This is not easy work. The sheepfold offers people great comfort and safety. Those called into shepherding are "to have great concern and to act with all speed, discernment, and diligence in order not to lose any of the sheep entrusted to [them]" (RB, 27.5). Not all people are alike; they bring differing personalities, gifts, and levels of spiritual maturity into the practice of spiritual direction. Benedict encourages the practice of adaptability within the flock. "He must so accommodate and adapt himself to each one's character and intelligence that he will not only keep the flock entrusted to his care from dwindling, but will rejoice in the increase of a good flock" (RB, 2.32).

TRAIN PEOPLE FROM SCRIPTURE. The *Rule* recommends training people in shepherding. Such a shepherd needs "to be learned in divine law, so that he has a treasury of knowledge" (RB, 64.9). One of the primary tasks for pastors who work with lay leaders involves the regular study and life application of Scripture, depositing wisdom from the Bible into the lives of shepherds. The work of Scripture instruction includes hearing, reading, studying, memorizing, and meditating upon the Word. At Community Presbyterian Church we do this together monthly. The ultimate goal is to be transformed by the Word of God by allowing our lives to be shaped by Christ through attentiveness to Scripture. As shepherds of God's people hold their lives accountable to Scripture, together they will increase their ability to care for others with wisdom and grace.

EMPHASIZE COMPASSION. Shepherds of souls are trained in the ministry of compassion. "Mercy triumphs over judgment" (Jas. 2:13b). Servant-leaders are called to care for hurting, needy people in the grace of Jesus Christ, extending God's mercy to God's people. Shepherds are to be chosen because they are "chaste, temperate, and merciful" (see RB, 64.9). Through regular instruction, such lay caregivers seek to embody the character of Jesus Christ, practicing a Christlike lifestyle nurtured through example and ongoing instruction from Scripture. Shepherding God's people means that we "must hate faults but love the brothers" (RB, 64.11). This way of shepherding calls us deeper, into a Christlike way of love that looks past the external actions into the heart of God; thus servant-leaders are better able to look with God's love into the hearts of people.

EXERCISE GENTLENESS IN DEALING WITH FAULTS. Shepherding involves wisdom in how to handle the faults of others, especially as these faults influence the life of the community. Benedict instructs his leaders to "use prudence and avoid extremes" (RB, 64.12). Rather than allow faults to flourish like weeds, he encourages the caregiver to "prune them away with prudence and love as he sees best for each individual" (RB, 64.14). Such gentleness and personal love in the face of the faults of others is the mark of wise shepherding within the community.

PRACTICE WHAT WE PREACH. Benedict tells leaders to practice what they preach. People do not want platitudes. They are looking for love and wisdom revealed more through character than by words. Shepherds of God's people are called to help others develop a whole new way of life. As Paul writes, "Therefore, if anyone is in Christ, he is a new creation; the old has gone, the new has come" (2 Cor. 5:17). In the process, lay leaders and professional ministers must be willing to let their own lives be spiritually transformed as well. Ultimately, every leader will stand before the Lord and "give God an account of all his judgments" (RB, 65.22). Even those who are not directly involved with leadership within a local church can learn from the practical wisdom of the *Rule* as expressed in this chapter. All people of faith are called to humbly step into the ministry of caring for the lives of others, seeking to offer wisdom, discernment, and love to the people of God in the practice of spiritual guidance.

SPIRITUAL ADMONITION

One of the most neglected aspects of spiritual guidance in the contemporary church is the ministry of spiritual admonition. According to Thomas Oden in his book *Pastoral Theology*:

> On the whole . . . it seems clear that the admonitory function of the modern pastor has been relatively neglected. In the interest of an overweening ethic of toleration, the pastor more and more has appeared in public view as one who dares not offend or appear "judgmental."

Oden offers several reasons for the neglect of the ministry of admonition, including "unconstrained individual freedom," "individual hedonic self-actualization," and "frenetic self-improvement strategies." In a culture that elevates individual freedom above communal responsibility, the gentle voice of admonition and the practice of accountability are often lost among the powerful influences of commercialism, hedonism, and consumerism. Marketing, electronic entertainment, and materialistic pursuits often have greater influence upon Christians today than Scripture or wise guidance. As Oden writes, "In modern society we have permitted a 'pass the buck' attitude toward moral accountability, social obligation, and personal duty." Secular and cultural influences seep into the life of the local church, decreasing the impact of Scripture, Christian community, or Christian leadership in the process of spiritual formation.

The life of a monk was to be lived in a community where every individual was held accountable for actions and intentions by the community on a daily basis, under the guidance of a mentor. Twelve of Benedict's seventy-three chapters in the *Rule* relate to admonition, including chapters 23–30 and 43–46. The underlying assumption in all of these chapters is that we need accountability in a loving community. On his first visit to the United States in April 2008, Pope Benedict XVI described the countercultural aspect of being a follower of Jesus in America.

> In a society which values personal freedom and autonomy, it is easy to lose sight of our dependence on others as well as the responsibilities that we bear toward them. . . . We were created as social beings who find fulfillment only in love—for God and for our neighbor.

Fifteen centuries earlier, Benedict of Nursia also viewed the call of Christ as countercultural, calling people out of a self-centered life into a life of loving accountability. Benedict believed all humans to be "stubborn or disobedient or proud" (see RB, 23.1). Even those living in a community will sometimes complain and grumble about the plans of their spiritual leaders. People are prone to make mistakes and overstep boundaries even when living in a faith community.

Benedict offers a wide variety of approaches to admonishment: encouragement, Scripture readings, private and public warnings, confession, removal of privileges, making amends, accountability, and discipline by temporary removal from the community. As any wise parent knows, "There ought to be due proportion between the seriousness of a fault and the measure of . . . discipline" (RB, 24.1). Lesser faults require lesser forms of admonition. More serious faults are treated with greater severity. The leader "determines the gravity of faults" (RB, 24.2). The heart of admonition, according to Benedict, is care and concern for the sick, not "tyranny over the healthy" (see RB, 27.6).

Because of abuses from overly zealous leaders who have tyrannized people with legalistic or excessive forms of admonition, some people have come to believe that the exercise of admonition has no place in the practice of spirituality today. But Thomas Oden challenges this assumption, declaring that "the long-standing neglect of church discipline and pastoral admonition leads to a breakdown and demoralization of Christian community." Benedictine formation does not allow the community to avoid the vital ministry of admonition, but asks leaders to discern the middle way between toleration and tyranny. Benedict offered monks multiple opportunities to turn their lives around, reform, or seek readmission into the monastery if they have abandoned the monastic life. Instead of avoiding admonition through excessive toleration, or abusing admonition through excessive discipline, Christian formation calls the local church into an "implicit trust of both parties toward each other."

Of the gift of mutual trust between a leader and a parishioner, Oden writes, "One member of the body of Christ looks to another to help grasp where the misdeeds or misjudgments may lie, in order to mature more fully toward humanity in Christ." People may still resist such loving admonishment with defensiveness or stonewalling. According to Oden, the practice of admonition in the local church today "hinges just here: learning precisely how to penetrate that defensiveness, but do it in a patient, caring, empathetic way so that in time the wrong can be righted and the person reconciled. This requires deep grounding in a 'love that covers a multitude of sins' (1 Pet. 4:8b)." Spiritual leaders today discover the middle way when they are motivated by love and prayer as they walk alongside those who need the ministry of admonition. As Benedict states, *"Let love for him be reaffirmed* (2 Cor. 2:8), and let all pray for him" (RB, 27.4).

THE ART OF SPIRITUAL DIRECTION

We have several artist friends who have converted their homes into art studios. I love going into these homes and seeing the latest works of art, even the unfinished works still in progress. We too are unfinished works in progress. One of the images used by Benedict for Christian formation is that of an artist workshop. As we heard in chapter two, within this studio a variety of tools are employed in the art of spiritual direction. Every art form requires the use of a variety of tools. Though the term "spiritual direction" does not appear in the *Rule*, the principles and daily practice of what has become known as spiritual direction can easily be gleaned from this guidebook. When speaking of spiritual direction, I include formal direction with a certified spiritual director, guidance from a pastor, priest, elder, or deacon, and also informal support between friends who regularly meet together to grow in a life of faith. Beyond one-on-one relationships, the art of spiritual direction may also be practiced within a small group setting, with the group leader facilitating growth in Christ among members of the group. In this section, I first want to review several images Benedict uses for guidance, applying these to the practice of spiritual direction. Next, I will review some basic qualifications for directors. Finally, I will examine tools of spiritual direction that may help us improve how we guide the lives of others.

CHRIST OUR SPIRITUAL DIRECTOR. The first and highest image for direction is found in the person of Jesus—the beginning and end of all Christian formation. The primary role of a spiritual director is to be an example of Christ to others who are seeking guidance for their lives. Benedict writes of the role of the abbot, "He is to imitate the loving example of the Good Shepherd" (RB, 27.8). All spiritual direction draws upon the example of Christ, as we seek to offer people the care of the Good Shepherd as expressed earlier in this chapter. At Community Presbyterian Church, our vision statement is to "know Christ and grow in Christ together." We are seeking to live out this Christ-centered vision by imitating Jesus in all our relationships, including those people seeking guidance from our community.

SPIRITUAL DIRECTION AS GARDENING. Another Benedictine image for spiritual director is that of a gardener tending his garden. "He should not gloss over the sins of those who err, but cut them out while he can, as soon as they begin to sprout" (RB, 2.26). This metaphor offers us a fruitful way of discussing growth in Christ, including preparation of the soil, planting of seeds, weeding, watering, and waiting. In this image, the sun and rain express the provision of God, who "causes his sun to rise on the evil and the good, and sends rain on the righteous and the unrighteous" (Matt. 5:45). The marvel and wonder of growth is seen in progressive stages of germination, sprouting, budding, flowering, and fruitfulness in our life in Christ. These stages of growth in the garden offer an excellent approach to evaluating growth in our lives and in the lives of those we are directing. Try asking such questions as follow: What good seeds have been planted in your life this past month? Where do you currently see signs of new growth in your garden? What weeds need to be pulled? How might your life be pruned to remove areas that have not been bearing any fruit? How might your life become more fruitful?

SPIRITUAL DIRECTION AS HEALTH CARE. Another metaphor for spiritual direction in the *Rule* is drawn from the health care profession. Since I'm married to a registered nurse, I value quality health care and those who help provide such care in our community. The spiritual director, as a wise health-care provider, is asked to "exercise the utmost care and concern for wayward brothers, because *it is not the healthy who need a physician, but the sick* (Matt. 9:12)" (RB, 27.1). In addition to physicians, there are other medical support staff in the medical community who also seek the optimal health of the client. The same is true of the spiritual community, with pastors, elders, deacons, and other spiritual health-care providers all looking for the best ways to bring healing and wellness to others. "He ought to use every skill of a wise physician and send in . . . mature and wise brothers who, under the cloak of secrecy, may support the wavering brother, urge him to be humble . . . and console him" (RB, 27.2–3). In this approach to spiritual direction, the local community of faith is viewed like a medical center where people come to receive spiritual wellness. According to Benedict, a spiritual health-care provider "should realize that he has undertaken care of the sick" (RB, 27.6). Continuing this medical metaphor, Benedict recommends a variety of remedies available for spiritual directors:

> After he has applied compresses, the ointment of encouragement, the medicine of divine Scripture . . . if he then perceives that his earnest efforts are unavailing, let him apply an even better remedy: he and all the brothers should pray for him so that the Lord, who can do all things, may bring about the health of the sick brother. (RB, 28.3–5)

Confidentiality is just as essential in spiritual direction as in the health care profession. Every spiritual director is tempted at times to share with others what they have heard behind closed doors— sometimes this is out of need for another opinion in a difficult situation. When a spiritual director maintains the integrity of confidentiality, she guards a person's privacy, providing a safe space where true healing can take place, "without exposing them and making them public" (RB, 46.6).

FINDING A SPIRITUAL DIRECTOR. What should we look for when seeking a spiritual guide or mentor? Benedict offers wisdom concerning the right qualifications to be found in a spiritual director. In his lifetime, he provided guidance for hundreds of believers under his care, and through his *Rule*, he has continued to guide hundreds of thousands of Christians through the centuries. What should I look for in a wise spiritual director?

QUALITIES TO LOOK FOR IN A SPIRITUAL DIRECTOR:

- Find someone who loves as Christ loves and teaches as Christ teaches. "He is believed to hold the place of Christ. . . . Never teach or decree or command anything that would deviate from the Lord's instructions" (RB, 2.2, 4).
- A spiritual director should guide not only through words but by example. "He must point out to them all that is good and holy more by example than by words . . . demonstrating God's instructions . . . by a living example" (RB, 2.12).
- Good spiritual mentors are willing to use both firm and gentle approaches to spiritual formation, depending on multiple factors, including the level of trust that has been

developed, personality types, and nature of the challenges being faced. As Benedict writes, *"Use argument, appeal, and reproof* (2 Tim. 4:2). Vary with circumstances . . . stern as a taskmaster, devoted and tender as only a father can be" (RB, 2.23–24).

- Mature spiritual directors are also not afraid to face dark troubles and spiritual sickness in a person. I believe these troubles and sickness should be faced by people who know they are loved and have the protection and support of others as they begin to face such troubles. "He should not gloss over the sins of those who err, but cut them out while he can" (RB, 2.26).

- Avoid a cookie-cutter approach to guiding others, but look for someone who treats each pilgrim as a unique and highly valued person—someone who is alert and sensitive to individual personalities, abilities, and spiritual gifts. "He must accommodate and adapt himself to each one's character and intelligence" (RB, 2.32).

- Look for people who understand they are guiding and caring for immortal souls. "He must know what a difficult and demanding burden he has undertaken: directing souls. . . . He should keep in mind that he has undertaken the care of souls for whom he must give an account" (RB, 2.31, 34).

- Excellent spiritual directors hold themselves accountable to God, and practice the art of spiritual direction with humility. Benedict offered warnings to spiritual leaders: "He must not show too great concern for the fleeting and temporal things of this world, neglecting or treating lightly the welfare of those entrusted to him. . . . Let him realize that on judgment day he will surely have to submit a reckoning to the Lord for all their souls" (RB, 2.33, 38).

- When looking for a spiritual director, consider the people you currently know who are living examples of some of the qualities above. If no one comes to mind, ask the wisest people you know in your circle of friends for referrals. Ask your local pastor or priest for spiritual direction. Also, consider going on a monastic retreat, and seeking spiritual direction from a monastic. Finally, you might look up Spiritual Directors International for listings of spiritual directors in a city nearest your home (see www .sdiworld.org).

Within the workshop of a community of faith, Benedict recommends a variety of tools for the practice of the art of spiritual direction. Below, I've highlighted four of these.

USE SCRIPTURE IN SPIRITUAL DIRECTION. First, we pick up the double-edged sword of God's Word. "For the word of God is living and active. Sharper than any double-edged sword, it penetrates even to dividing soul and spirit, joints and marrow; it judges the thoughts and attitudes of the heart" (Heb. 4:12). Practically speaking, all Christian guidance is based upon Scripture, and as spiritual directors, we must be willing to be trained in Scripture, including regular reading, study, memorization, and meditation upon God's Word. Whenever I'm with a person for spiritual direction, I have a Bible on the table, and simultaneously seek to listen to the person while tuning in to God's Spirit and Word. Out of this abundance of the treasury of knowledge, we approach the practice of directing others. Benedict warns directors to "never teach or decree or command anything that would deviate from the Lord's instructions" (RB, 2.4). With the Word of God in our heart, we gently proceed to become involved in people's personal lives, entering into the realm of soul and spirit, as we seek to understand and help direct the thoughts and attitudes of the heart.

GUIDE WITH HUMILITY AND ACCOUNTABILITY. A twin set of tools for spiritual direction in Benedictine spirituality are humility and accountability. People are attracted to power. The *Rule* counters the human tendency to grasp for power through extolling the virtue of humility and the daily practice of accountability in community. All believers are ultimately accountable to God. This is especially important for those seeking to offer direction. "[He] should keep in mind that he has undertaken the care of souls for whom he must give an account" (RB, 2.34, also 37). From this eternal perspective spiritual directors enter into the experiences of others with humility, staying as close as they can to God's heart and God's Word.

EXERCISE DISCERNMENT. Another tool in Benedict's approach to spiritual direction is the practice of discernment. His first biographer, Gregory the Great, described Benedict's *Rule* as "outstanding in its discernment." As Markus comments, "For Gregory, that true artist in the 'art of arts, the governing of souls,' [discernment] was the key to the spiritual life." In directing people, a spiritual director "should be discerning and moderate, bearing in mind the discretion of holy Jacob, who said: *If I drive my flocks too hard, they will all die in a single day* (Gen. 33:13)" (RB, 64.17–18). Discernment means to *sift through* or *separate away*: Latin: *discernere*, from *dis* (away) and *cernere* (separate); Greek: *diakrino*, from *dia* (through) and *krino* (judge or sift). The work of discernment calls us to sit with other people as they "sift through" the details, memories, feelings, and stories, looking for the wheat while sifting out the chaff. "Point out to them all that is good and holy more by example than by words" (RB, 2.12). People love telling and hearing stories. Ask questions that help people sift through their story, as you listen for what is "good and holy."

KEEP LOVE AT THE HEART. The final tool of spiritual direction is love. As Margaret Guenther writes, "The amateur is a lover. Love impels her work and lies at its heart. Spiritual direction, as a work of love, is also a work of freedom. The director is willing to let be, to love with an open hand. Hers is a contemplative love." As a practical way of expressing this love in a community, Benedict warns against favoritism. "Avoid all favoritism. . . . He is not to love one more than another" (RB, 2.16–17). We enter this ministry with humility and compassion, knowing that Christ alone can lead another toward maturity. Spiritual direction means living a life of love in relationship with others; loving people as Christ loves us, "with an open hand." Since we are unfinished works of art, we can be "confident of this that he who began a good work in [us] will carry it on to completion until the day of Christ Jesus" (Phil. 1:6).

TAKING STEPS
INTO CHRISTIAN FORMATION

from Chapter Four

- If you do not serve as a leader within your local congregation, consider ways to encourage those who do. For example, pray regularly for them by name; also, tell them what you appreciate about their service for the Lord as a servant-leader.

- If you currently serve in leadership within a local church, commit yourself to recruiting a few others who can assist you. Train them to do what you do, and trust them to carry out the work of spiritual leadership.

- Attend training sessions for learning how to better care for peoples' lives, including personal and spiritual growth in Christ. Learn to shepherd and care for God's people. If you are already active in a caring ministry, consider offering courses or one-on-one mentoring for others who may be interested in learning to shepherd people. Study passages together with others from the Bible that speak of caring for people, shepherding people's lives, and pastoral care in God's church.

- Ask a good friend to give you the gift of admonition, including encouragement, truths from Scripture, private warnings and exhortations, a willingness to hear personal confession of sin, and loving accountability.

- Find a spiritual director with whom you will meet at least monthly for spiritual guidance.

- Become a mentor to another person, offering them spiritual guidance through regular meetings for spiritual growth.

CHAPTER 5

The Path of Ordinary Spirituality

According to Karen MacNeil, author of *The Wine Bible*, Dom Pierre Perignon invented champagne. Though wine had been produced in the Champagne region of France since Roman times, it was not until the end of the seventeenth century that the product we now know as champagne was first created. Dom Perignon Champagne enjoys a worldwide reputation for excellence in sparkling wines. Two facts stand out about this man. First, Dom Perignon did not drink alcohol. Second, he was a Benedictine monk. Though he was unusual in being a teetotaling French monk, he was not unusual in his view of work. In a Benedictine monastery, work is prayer. *Ora et labora*, "pray and work": this is the Latin phrase that has come to summarize the Benedictine way of life. As mentioned before, prayer is the work of a Benedictine monk. Similarly, monks offer their manual labor as a prayerful gift to the Lord. The work of our body is an extension of the work of our spirit. *The Wine Bible* offers a unique insight into the Dom Perignon work ethic in producing such an excellent product as champagne:

> Perignon was an avid winemaker and savvy businessman. He increased both the size of the abbey's vineyard holdings and the value of the wine produced. By 1700 the wines of Hautvillers

were worth four times that of basic Champagne. . . . Perignon was fanatical about consistency, precision, and discipline in grape growing and winemaking. He insisted that vines be pruned severely and only sparingly fertilized, thus lowering the yield of each grapevine and improving the concentration of the wine. . . . That the world's most notorious "seduction wine" should have been the brainchild of a monk is described by the British wine writer Nicholas Faith as "an agreeable paradox."

Inherent in Perignon's view of the spiritual life is "an agreeable paradox": the extraordinary is discovered in the ordinary. There is very little "flash in the pan" excitement about Benedictine spirituality. The truly radical aspect of Benedict's vision of Christian formation is that it is ordinary. What makes it attractive, I believe, is the sensible, down-to-earth understanding of spiritual life in which God is just as present when we wash dishes and weed the garden as he is when we pray the Psalms or kneel before the Eucharist. Dom Perignon is a classic example of ordinary spirituality. He devoted his life to God through the daily details of manual labor in a vineyard and cultivated world-class excellence in sparkling wine. Perignon reveals in his life the true nature of ordinary spirituality. We are called to reveal the glory of God through living with excellence in the mundane places of life.

Benedictine spirituality invites us to see all of life as sacred. God loves to meet with us in the ordinary places of our daily life together. When followers of Christ take the incarnation of Christ as seriously as Benedict did, they begin to view all life as sacred, for Christ chose to humble himself, dwell among us in the mundane places of our daily life. The Christian life is much more than rare transcendent experiences or once-in-a-lifetime mystical encounters. For Benedict, the spiritual life is discovered in the ordinary daily rhythms of life, in families, in the kitchen, at work, and at play.

BECOMING LIKE CHILDREN

Adults often take special delight in the presence of children at play, whether in playgrounds, parks, or along the beach; whether building a fort, playing tag, or deep in the world of their own imaginations, Children naturally know how to play. No one needs to teach them to use their imagination, create new games, and take delight in the world. Dr. Jeff Sigafoos, professor of education at the University of Tasmania, makes the following remark about children: "Play is the business of childhood, and it would be fair to say that most children love their job."

Jesus declared that unless we change and become like little children, we will not enter the kingdom of heaven (Matt. 18:3). God invites us to change our way of looking at life and to become like little children. Part of this new way of living is a playful invitation into life with God in this present moment. Children take delight in this day and this moment. Ordinary spirituality sees today as the time and place where we meet God. The beginning of ordinary spirituality is simply a childlike trust in our heavenly Father, who knows what we need long before we ask. Ordinary spirituality opens us into a whole new way of living, a more playful and prayerful, childlike way of life.

In the sixth century, the monastery also served as an orphanage and training school for children. Few other places in medieval society would receive unwanted children. No other place in Benedict's time taught poor children to read. Both poor and rich alike presented their children to the monastery for various social and economic reasons. The presentation of children to the monastery was called an *oblatione* (see RB, 59.8), or an offering of a gift. Children were seen as a gift from God to be raised, trained, and cared for with the same love that wise parents provide for their own blood children.

Though children no longer inhabit Benedictine monasteries, guests to monasteries still sense a childlike joy among Benedictine monks. Monks whistle merry songs as they work in the garden, smile and wave at guests in the guesthouse, and seem very willing to share an amusing story with a guest on retreat. During many retreats to monasteries, I've often heard laughter coming from a bench in the garden where a monk was meeting with a guest for spiritual direction. With Christ at the center, Benedictine spirituality offers people a childlike delight in life even in the face of pain and suffering. This childlike approach to life includes playfulness, taking delight in simple pleasures of life, as well as a humble, daily trust in our heavenly Father, who will provide all we need. Just as little children worry very little about the source of their evening meal, due to the structure of the monastery, monks worry very little about food. Through the simplicity and childlike nature of Benedictine spirituality, the mundane tasks of manual labor become one more way to delight in the provision of a heavenly Father.

TABLE TALK

Food preparation is one of the most essential of our daily tasks, simply because we all must eat. Even with this necessity in mind, it still may come as a bit of a surprise that Benedict would devote so much attention to food service in one of the most influential spiritual classics ever written. Personally, I appreciate the real-life practicality of a guidebook for the spiritual life that includes details regarding food preparation, kitchen service, meal times, and the proper amount of food and beverage to be served daily. He carefully describes the head of food services in the monastery, the cellarer, as someone who is "wise, mature in conduct, temperate, not an excessive eater, not proud, excitable, offensive, dilatory, or wasteful, but God-fearing, and like a father to the whole community" (RB, 31.2). Cellarer in Latin is *cellararius*, derived from the Latin word for cellar, the room below ground for long-term storage of wine and foods.

Dom Perignon was a cellarer. Soon after he arrived at the Benedictine abbey of Hautvilliers, France, in 1668, at the age of twenty-nine, he was placed in charge of the food service for the entire community. Of course, such a post included the production of wine for the table, a task to which Perignon excelled. But Dom Perignon's tasks extended far beyond the vineyards. Like contemporary corporate food service managers, the cellarer was in charge of scheduling kitchen duties; managing menus and storerooms; overseeing all food production, including those food products bound for market to support the monastery; all shipping and receiving; as well as the daily bartering with other merchants for the goods that the monastery was unable to produce themselves. Knowing the task of the cellarer to be very complex, Benedict wrote, "If the community is rather large, he should be given helpers, that with their assistance he may calmly perform the duties of his office" (RB, 31.17). Underlying this demanding position within the community is the virtue of humility. The cellarer is asked to imitate Jesus, who stooped low to fit into our humble frame. "Above all, let him [the cellarer] be humble. If goods are not available to meet a request, he will offer a kind word in reply" (RB, 31.13). The bottom line for the cellarer was to produce basic life support for monks; both physical and spiritual nourishment. "He will provide the brothers their allotted amount of food without any pride or delay" (RB, 31.16).

Today, food service mostly happens within homes or institutions. The local church falls somewhere in between these two by providing a spiritual home and family within an institutional setting. The style and extent of food service within the local church is often determined by the size of the kitchen and serving area, not by any spiritual principle. With Benedict as our guide, we can step into this most ordinary of places, the kitchen, and review how people are spiritually cared for and nurtured through the giving and receiving of nourishment.

In the midst of his chapters on ordinary spirituality, Benedict writes one of the most astonishing sentences found in classic writings on the Christian life. "[The cellarer] will regard all utensils and goods of the monastery as sacred vessels of the altar, aware that nothing is to be neglected" (RB, 31.10–11). Are we to place the common kitchen measuring cup on the same level of importance as the communion chalice? Do garden tools, such as rakes and hoses, carry the same holy status as pulpits and baptismal fonts? Benedictine formation affirms that every part of our lives are sacred, including measuring cups and garden tools. There is to be no distinction between ordinary life and sacramental life. All tools are to be regarded as sacred, because all life is sacramental. "Nothing is to be neglected." Remember that Benedict was a lay monk. The *Rule* is surprisingly lacking in priestly directions and sacramental language. The sacraments are seldom mentioned in the *Rule*. Benedictine scholar Timothy Fry describes the scarcity of references to the Eucharist in the *Rule* as somewhat scandalous. "The term *eucharistia* never appears in [the *Rule*]." Though the formal sacraments of the church are hardly mentioned in the *Rule*, the daily life and work of the monk, including the ordinary tools to be used for this work, were viewed by Benedict as sacred.

I believe this lack of references to the sacraments in the *Rule* may be best understood when we discover Benedict's sacramental view of ordinary life. Every day involves many sacramental acts, such as tending vines in the vineyard, doing laundry, and cleaning up after the evening meal. Benedict understood all life as sacramental, including such mundane tasks as hoeing weeds in the garden.

A thousand years before John Calvin declared even the most menial work as potentially glorifying to God, Benedict proclaimed the utensils of the kitchen, garden, and toolshed as holy as the "sacred vessels of the altar." Monks are called primarily to pray and work, but they need to eat properly in order to work and pray effectively. For Benedict, all work is sacred. Healthy monks are better able to glorify God than sick monks. Benedict offers a down-to-earth vision of Christian formation that astonishes people today just as it did when these words were first written. In this vision of ordinary spirituality, body and spirit are not viewed as competitors, but colaborers in the holy work of formation into the wholeness of Jesus Christ.

What might all this mean for us today? A sacramental view of life causes us to see the brilliant glory of God shining out from every corner of our daily living. When a person first understands that all life is sacramental and reveals the glory and splendor of God, the smallest and most mundane tasks are seen in a new light, in the light of eternity. As C.S. Lewis describes it in *The Screwtape Letters*, "The Present is the point at which time touches eternity. . . . The Present is all lit up with eternal rays." It is in living fully for God in the present, with whatever task is at hand, that we discover the genius of Benedict's vision for Christian formation. The surprise realization dawns upon us that God truly is with us, smiling upon us, inspiring us in "whatever [we] do, whether in word or deed," whether in a church sanctuary or in the kitchen, to "do it all in the name of the Lord Jesus, giving thanks to God the Father through him" (Col. 3:17).

TOOLS AND WORK

It has always seemed odd to me when I have been on retreat at a monastery to see a monk operating a backhoe or a chainsaw. In just another hour, the same fellow will be standing in a white robe in a choir stall singing the Psalms. The Benedictine view of faith involves a lifestyle of stewardship. We are not owners of the earth but rather stewards and caretakers of every provision from God. As Benedict writes in the *Rule*,

> The goods of the monastery, that is, its tools, clothing, or anything else, should be entrusted to brothers whom the abbot appoints and in whose manner of life he has confidence. He will, as he sees fit, issue to them the various articles to be cared for and collected after use. (RB, 32.1–2)

These sentences lay out the basic plan for stewardship in community, which includes the delegation of authority to worthy stewards, the distribution of items to people, and the collection of these items after the people have finished with them. The items are held in common trust for all the people. Benedict warns against carelessness in the use of tools and goods, such as failing to clean a garment or neglecting to sharpen an axe after use. One of the classic stories from Gregory's *Life and Miracles of St. Benedict* involved a brother using a tool to trim brush by a lake in preparation of planting a garden. While the tool was in use, the iron blade flew off the handle into the lake and sank. Benedict miraculously recovered the iron blade and told the brother not to be upset but to continue with his work.

Today, people of faith still struggle with issues regarding the use of tools and material goods. Too often, we allow our private way of thinking to govern who is allowed to have access to our tools and possessions. Does everyone in a faith community need to own their own washer, dryer, ladder, and set of power tools? Why not consider ways to create a common pool of tools that is available for all involved within a particular community? The local church is one of the places in society today where people actually share material goods in a common, shared life. Churches tend to hold in common the property and contents within the church buildings, setting policies and plans for faithful care of these items entrusted to them by God.

When Community Presbyterian Church was remodeled in 1997, I received a new pastor's study. When I moved into this space, I thought about how the layout of the room might assist the work of study, prayer, welcoming people, and caring for people. My desk does not stand between me and people who come into the room, but rather it sits at an angle that allows me a straight path to welcome all who enter the room. A small couch and several comfortable chairs surround a wood coffee table. The walls are lined with bookshelves. Overhead, we installed a beautiful lamp made of stained glass art—a beautiful knotted Celtic cross my dad made for me. Standing lamps sit in several corners. Whenever new people come into this study, they comment on how warm and welcoming it feels. Benedictine spirituality of work as prayer has deeply influenced my understanding of work. This includes the design of a pastor's study.

Monastic spirituality can also influence how a congregation views the church building and its grounds. Everything belongs to the Lord. We are stewards of God's treasures. Every tool, including the communion chalice and the garden rake, are to be regarded as sacred. The church is people, not buildings; yet we are called to care for buildings and gardens, and "nothing is to be neglected," including the storing of garden rakes, and the placement of tables. Church trustees, building and grounds committees, and other church property stewards are easily overlooked and often taken for granted within a local church. Anyone who has served in such capacities knows the challenges of caring for the goods and items within a faith community. While stewards graciously tend to the many details of upkeep of property, idle onlookers sometimes fall into complaining and grumbling about the list of fix-it jobs still left undone, or about misplaced objects, broken dishes, and "it's not the way it used to be." Some of Benedict's most severe warnings in the *Rule* are against the sin of grumbling. Better to step in and serve with gratitude than step back and complain.

Benedict considered idleness "the enemy of the soul" (see RB, 48.1). As a result, the monastic day follows a set structure alternating between work and prayer. Alongside the seven times a day of communal prayer, a monk gives four to six hours a day for manual labor "at whatever work needs to be done" (see RB, 48.3). The only exception is Sunday, when monks celebrate a Sabbath rest from their physical toil. Some forms of work continue on Sunday, such as food service and guest services. Benedict fought against the prevalent Mediterranean view in his day when he viewed manual labor as a blessing from God, essential for human health and maturity. Work was not just for slaves and the poor. Benedict refused to bend to the aristocratic culture of Roman society that prided itself on being above manual labor. Benedict wove a daily work ethic into the very fabric of the *Rule*. "When they live by the labor of their hands . . . then they are really monks" (RB, 48.8). The manual labor of the monastery enabled working monks to raise sufficient income to support the entire monastic community and have a surplus to serve the poor beyond the walls of the monastery. Regarding Benedict's understanding of manual labor, Fry notes,

> St. Benedict looks upon work in a highly traditional way: its purposes are to provide a means of subsistence for the monks themselves, to be an ascetical discipline in harmony with the rest of their life, and to produce a surplus for almsgiving to the poor. There was a great concern for the unfortunate, for travelers and guests, who were to be received as Christ.

In this efficient system of communal labor, Benedictine monks planted orchards and vineyards, hand copied hundreds of thousands of biblical manuscripts, founded and maintained most of the first libraries of Europe, created crafts guilds that birthed the artisan middle class of medieval Europe, dug wells, and built irrigation systems interlacing much of Europe. These gifts of Benedictine work supported and nurtured thousands of villages and towns clustered around the stable influence of daily manual labor within the cloister. Gerald Sittser provides this summary of the impact of cenobitic monastic work upon Western Europe:

> Monasteries once owned large tracks of land, and the monks turned that land into prosperous farms, ranches, and vineyards. Monks became masters of skilled trades too, and they put those trades to good use, producing items like furniture, wine, and cloth. Monks copied, illuminated, catalogued, and stored manuscripts in large libraries. They collected paintings, mosaics, sculptures, relics, and other cultural artifacts, established schools to teach people to read and write, and deployed missionaries to win barbarian groups to

Christianity, thus helping to evangelize Western Europe during its darkest years. In short, monasteries preserved and spread the cultural heritage of Western civilization. We are profoundly indebted to these institutions for preserving this legacy.

MATERIAL POSSESSIONS

What does Christian formation have to say about material possessions? How much is enough? Within contemporary middle-class culture, valuable economic lessons can be learned from Benedictine formation. Benedict declared private ownership a most "evil practice," a practice that he declared "must be uprooted and removed from the monastery" (see RB, 33.1). Today, such a view looks extreme, if not dangerous. Yet, we often participate in public ownership in many realms of daily life without giving it much thought. A few examples include city parks, city libraries, neighborhood playgrounds, local public schools, public radio and television, public highways, roads and bridges, public beaches, and national parks. Many people use these facilities, though they own none of them privately. Often, a branch of government or a nonprofit organization manages the shared public resource. Without these realms, our lives would be significantly diminished.

As followers of Jesus Christ, we believe we do not ultimately own anything, but rather we are stewards of the gifts God has entrusted into our care. This stewardship includes our physical bodies. "You are not your own; you were bought at a price. Therefore honor God with your body" (1 Cor. 6:19c–20). While few of us are destined to become monks, anyone who has been active in a local congregation already understands the principle of stewardship. Churches, on behalf of all the people, hold in common the church property, including all the contents of the church building, for the use of all the people.

An issue came up several years ago in the church where I serve regarding the setup of the Fellowship Hall. This hall is used every week by dozens of different groups—so how it is set up involves a high potential for tension. At a regular monthly meeting of the elders, a heated discussion broke out over this issue. After listening for some time to the discussion, I offered a theology of stewardship, declaring that all objects in the church building belonged to God alone, and we were all stewards of all God's treasures, including forks, spoons, and tables. Christians today have much to learn from our monastic brothers and sisters regarding stewardship of material possessions shared in common.

Twice in the *Rule* Benedict refers to the book of Acts, chapter four, citing the example of the early church regarding material possessions. "All the believers were one in heart and mind. No one claimed that any of his possessions was his own, but they shared everything they had . . . and it was distributed to anyone as he had need" (Acts 4:32, 35). The Christian journey into shared ownership begins with our faith in Christ and our relationship with others in the community of faith. Members of the early church described in Acts made the radical claim that nothing belonged to them, but everything belonged to God alone. Between the haves and have-nots, sharing took place, with plans set in place for the distribution of possessions to the needy (Acts 6:1–6). "Whoever needs less should thank God and not be distressed, but whoever needs more should feel humble because of his weakness, not self-important because of the kindness shown him" (RB, 34.3–4). Every community has those who need less and those who need more. Part of the joy of the life of faith is to follow in the footsteps of Jesus, who fed the hungry, healed the sick, and cared for the needy.

Such a way of life is no more evident than in the monastic kitchen or infirmary. "The brothers should serve one another. Consequently, no one will be excused from kitchen service ... for such service increases reward and fosters love" (RB, 35.1–2). Ordinary spirituality is most evident in loving service to the needy in the name of Jesus Christ, especially in such ordinary settings as washing dishes and caring for the sick. Benedict claimed that "[c]are of the sick must rank above and before all else, so that they may truly be served as Christ, for he said, *I was sick and you visited me* (Matt. 25:36)" (RB, 36.1–2). The parable Jesus told of the sheep and the goats moved Benedict to seek help for the hungry, the thirsty, the stranger, the naked, and the sick (Matt. 25:31–46). These groups of needy people are even more threatened when they are very young or very old. Thus, monastic compassion has always sought to make a difference in the lives of children and the elderly. "Since their lack of strength must always be taken into account" (RB, 37.2), special provisions should be made for the old and the young, including relaxing "the strictness of the rule with regard to food" (RB, 37.2), and encouraging the monks to treat children and seniors with extra kindness.

Anyone who lived through the 1950s may think this chapter reads like repackaged Marxist propaganda. Even though private ownership for Christians continues to present many challenges to formation in Christ, I am not advocating a life of voluntary poverty. Rather, Benedict invites us to take a serious look into the teachings of Scripture, especially as discovered in the book of Acts, and consider biblical approaches to spiritual formation, including the daily issues of common ownership in the midst of private ownership. The goal is to make a difference in this world for Christ through the sharing of the material possessions and assets that we have been given with those whose needs are far greater than our own.

Benedictine spirituality calls us to put our faith into action in the

daily places where we work, serve, and love. Spirituality is not primarily a once-in-a-lifetime, transcendent experience. It is not the
exclusive realm of gurus and mystics. Christian spirituality unfolds
in everyday life, among the dishes and diapers, at the school yard, and
in the office. How do we find God in such places? The *Rule* offers
a modest answer. Put love in action, especially on behalf of needy
people in our community and world.

In celebration of the path of "ordinary spirituality," I offer the following benediction: *May we become like children once again, learning to
play, trust, and live fully in the gift called today. May we see all life as
sacramental, welcoming the radiant presence of God in every ordinary
act and daily task. May we accept our work as a gift from God given for
the good of others as well as for our good, and may we faithfully carry
out the calling to which we have been called through daily labors. May
we all find joy in serving others by sharing from the abundance of what
we have been given with those whose needs are greater than our own.
Finally, may we celebrate God's goodness in the breaking of bread
and drinking the fruit of the vine until the kingdom of God is restored
in the fullness of joy.*

TAKING STEPS
INTO CHRISTIAN FORMATION
from Chapter Five

- Within your local church, help organize a group to go through storage areas in the church building to make an inventory of supplies and tools, and create a plan for better management of these items.

- Suggest that your group, your church, or your community seriously study what stewardship means and what changes in attitude and practice a biblical view of stewardship would require—both in material possessions and in your life together.

- If you have a hobby of making things with your hands, or growing things in your garden, practice your hobby this season with a commitment to excellence, doing what you do for Christ. Consider giving a gift from this hobby to someone in your church family or community.

- Offer a prayer of thanks while washing dishes, doing laundry, or weeding the garden. Bring your faith in Christ into one of the manual chores of ordinary living. Offer to wash dishes or vacuum the carpet at the church building for a month.

- Spend a whole day looking at all life as sacred. Focus upon details of the day as though they all are shining the splendor of God into your life. Write in a journal some of your insights gained from this "sacramental" day.

- Find a dozen objects in your home that are seldom used, and give them away to a thrift shop or needy family in your area.

- Volunteer at your local food pantry this month.

CHAPTER 6

The Path of Lectio Divina

The classic Benedictine practice of *lectio divina*, or sacred study of Scripture, provides the daily nourishment for those who journey along the way of Christ. The way Benedict chose to live fifteen hundred years ago included daily times for prayerful reading of Scripture. Though most other people were illiterate in sixth-century Italy, Benedict insisted that every monk, whether peasant or aristocrat, was taught to read and to practice the discipline of *lectio divina*—prayerfully reading Scripture several hours every day. Through this instruction, Benedictine monasteries developed libraries and literacy across the European continent during the medieval period, as they preserved biblical manuscripts and the classic literature of antiquity. As we walk together further into our life of faith, we come upon the "village" of *Lectio Divina*. In this chapter, we will explore together the Benedictine practice of sacred study of Scripture, including practical travel tips on how to carry this spiritual discipline on our pilgrimage of faith.

THE GIFT OF BOOKS

Over the past fifteen centuries, Benedictine monasteries have enjoyed daily time for reading. "Reading will always accompany the meals of the brothers" (RB, 38.1). Benedict also set aside two hours every day for private reading of Scripture. In order to fulfill this plan, manuscripts had to be produced for each monastery, and monks had to be taught to read. "Brothers will read . . . not according to rank, but according to their ability to benefit their hearers" (RB, 38.12).

Benedict's literacy plan centered upon reading for the sake of growth in Christ. Every monk was expected to learn to read in order to feed daily upon the Word of God. As a direct result of Benedict's daily reading plan, monastic libraries were birthed across the continent of Europe, preserving the great manuscripts of the ancient world. Nine hundred years before Johannes Gutenberg converted his winepress into the first moveable-type printing press, Benedictine monks were stocking the shelves of their libraries with thousands of manuscripts. These included multiple manuscripts of the books of the Bible as well as other classic works of antiquity.

When the *Rule* requires a monk to read each day, every other activity is to be laid aside and a monk is to focus all his attention upon this essential work. In many homes across the country, such daily reading time is known as "drop everything and read" or "D.E.A.R time." One of the greatest gifts parents and grandparents can give children is a love of learning through daily read-aloud time. In light of the growing presence of electronic media in the home, there is also a growing need for adults to take time to sit together with children to read aloud from a book. Besides reading aloud, children need to be encouraged to read books on their own. Professional educators have discovered that while most children are not being encouraged to read at home, when they are provided a time in the classroom for relaxed reading, attitudes toward reading improve along with vocabulary, comprehension, and other academic skills.

Many "thieves" have snuck into twenty-first-century homes to snatch up valuable reading time: television, computers, cell phones, and electronic games are at the top of the list of things most detrimental to the practice of taking daily reading time in the home. Few computer users today would consider operating their computers without installing a firewall and an antivirus program. Yet, many people have no such protection built into their daily life against threats to literacy. Spiritually minded parents call their families to meet together to agree on limits for computer and television use in the home to clear space for daily reading.

The first words found in the *Rule* are "listen carefully, my son" (RB, prologue 1). One of the key ways of listening in a monastery is through reading Scripture aloud. Benedict offers several settings in which daily reading takes place: reading aloud in the community during meal times, reading aloud during worship times, and reading in solitude in the morning and evening. Besides reading Scripture, Benedict recommends reading whatever "will benefit the hearers" (see RB, 42.3), including classic Christian writers from his era, such as John Cassian, Basil, and other saints of the church. Series of Christian spiritual classics covering the past two thousand years of writing are readily available from many publishing companies today. Here are a few examples of such writings:

- Paraclete Press, Christian Classics
- Paulist Press, The Classics of Western Spirituality
- Crossroad, The Spiritual Legacy Series
- Random House, The Vintage Spiritual Classics
- HarperCollins, HarperCollins Spiritual Classics

Each of these series of books translates the best writings of classic Christian spirituality into readable English and gives brief introductions to help contemporary readers better understand the context in which these authors lived, and the settings in which they wrote their works. Taking Benedict's recommendation for good books, Christian pilgrims are wise to obtain books on the lives of the saints. These include the classic *Butler's Lives of the Saints* (Paraclete Press, 2005), as well as such contemporary compilations as Robert Ellsberg's *All Saints: Daily Reflections on Saints, Prophets and Witnesses for Our Time* (Crossroad, 1997). Finally, anthologies of Christian classics offer helpful introductory approaches for beginning readers in Christian spirituality. One such volume, *Invitation to Christian Spirituality: An Ecumenical Anthology* (Oxford University Press, 1999), edited by John R. Tyson, provides brief biographies and excerpts from the writings of the ancient church, the medieval era, and the Reformation era, as well as from modern and contemporary spiritual writers. Any of these works will nourish a reader's mind and spirit, while expanding the horizons of all who desire to drink from the deep well of Christian spirituality. When discussing our faith with one another, we might simply ask, "What good books have you been reading?" We are wise not only to ask for good book recommendations that have helped to nourish the mind and spirit, but to read them and allow them to encourage our faith formation in Christ.

SILENCE AND SOLITUDE

Our journey with Christ is more about listening than speaking. On our family hikes in the Olympic National Park over the past decade, one of the strange wonders we discovered along the path after the first full day of hiking was the ubiquitous presence of silence. Every year our family returns to the silence of the Olympics, often hiking twenty or more miles away from civilization into the quiet wonder of creation. After a week of silence in the high country, the return to human civilization sometimes seems like an assault of human noise upon the ears.

One of the most difficult tasks in our walk of faith is learning to unwrap and practice the gift of silence. Whenever I return to the monastery, I delight in this gift, almost as if silence and solitude were water and bread to a thirsty, hungry soul. When fellow retreatants want to chat, I politely excuse myself and move into a quiet place where I can enjoy more silence. Benedict calls silence the "restraint of speech" (RB, 6). Anyone who desires to grow spiritually will eventually come to the crossroad of words and silence. At that junction, a critical choice must be made: do we continue down the path of words, or do we take the road less traveled—the way of restraint of speech? According to Benedict, "There are times when good words are to be left unsaid out of esteem for silence" (RB, 6.2).

How can we increase our appreciation of silence? Here are a few ideas. Place times of "elected silence" into your weekly rhythm of life. As Gerard Manley Hopkins wrote of this experience:

> Elected silence sing to me,
> and beat upon my whorle'd ear;
> pipe me to pastures still and be
> the music that I care to hear.

Daily, add a short period of "elected" silence, even five minutes, into your existing faith practice. Weekly, try adding a longer period of silence, such as an hour or two, either early in the morning or late at night. Annually, try getting away for a weekend of silence, where few words are spoken and few are heard. Following such a contemplative listening weekend, you may awaken with a different outlook on life— with the gift of listening blossoming in your life.

How will this practice help us to grow spiritually? When we are silent, we give up the need to be in control of others. We become listeners and learners. "Speaking and teaching are the master's task; the disciple is to be silent and listen" (RB, 6.6). Silence teaches us to listen, and this includes listening to God as well as listening to others. Learning to listen to God is one of the most important tasks for pilgrims. Silence also helps our willful hearts learn to yield to God. When we enter into silence, we let go of our need to control God through words, and become like a child, open to hear what our heavenly Father tells us.

Benedict calls for silence, not because he is opposed to words, but because he knows how powerful this spiritual discipline is for the formation of our life with Christ. There lies an inherent danger in the attempt to draw upon principles from the monastic cloister and put them into practice outside the walls of the monastery. The busy world of people requires us to use words. All the more, then, we are wise to heed the invitation into the sanctuary of silence, as the author of Ecclesiastes writes:

> Guard your steps when you go to the house of God. Go near to listen rather than to offer the sacrifice of fools, who do not know that they do wrong. Do not be quick with your mouth, do not be hasty in your heart to utter anything before God. God is in heaven and you are on earth, so let your words be few. (Eccl. 5:1–2)

Silence requires vigilance. We wander easily into the misuse of words. The Bible calls us to place a guard over our mouths. "Set a guard over my mouth, O LORD; keep watch over the door of my lips" (Ps. 141:3). Here are five practical ways we may "go near to listen," as we begin to learn the gift of silence.

RELY UPON A SPIRITUAL MENTOR. Only with the help of loving accountability can this discipline of silence grow in the life of a disciple. It may seem odd, but we must use words to grow in our practice of silence. We all need wise mentors who are willing to meet with us as students of the faith to discuss our use of words and our restraint of speech. Check in with one another and share your experiences. Even saints struggle with the many problems connected to the practice of silence. These are distractions, mental meanderings, confusion at hearing inner voices, discernment to know the voice of the Lord, as well as times of dryness where we sit in silence and feel nothing and hear nothing.

ASK A FRIEND TO HELP YOU LEARN SILENCE. Silence does not come easily to most people. We need help setting a guard over our mouths so that we can begin to listen. Why not ask a friend to help you learn silence? Try an experiment for one month in which you meet with this friend weekly to go over the "silence report." Share with your friend what you are learning about "going near to God to listen." Discover the wonder of resting in silence, and even occasionally, experiencing the joy of hearing the still, small voice of God, speaking with grace and truth to all who are willing to learn to listen. Such is the picture Benedict offers his readers during daily times of *lectio divina*. The sweetness of daily time in silence and solitude is so precious that he assigns "one or two seniors . . . to make rounds of the monastery while the brothers are reading. Their duty is to see that no brothers are so apathetic as to waste time or engage in idle talk to the neglect of his reading, and so not only harm himself but also distract others" (RB, 48.17–18). Every other week, I enjoy sitting for five minutes of silence during our Taizé worship services. What a blessing I've received from sharing times of silence in community, with other fellow pilgrims who are also learning to receive this gift.

LEARN SILENCE WHILE LYING IN BED. In addition to the daily times of solitude and silence for personal reading, Benedict also asserts that "monks should diligently cultivate silence at all times, but especially at night" (RB, 42). We spend one-third of our lives in bed. This time is precious for learning habits of the heart, especially the gift of silence. Once the tongue has been stilled, there still remains the deeper task of quieting the mind. The ninth step of humility in the *Rule* focuses upon learning inner silence. "The ninth step of humility is that a monk controls his tongue and remains silent, not speaking unless asked a question, for Scripture warns, *In a flood of words you will not avoid sinning* (Prov. 10:19)" (RB, 7.56–57). The Jesus Prayer, mentioned in chapter three, has been an excellent way of quieting my mind and spirit while lying in bed. When my mind is "worried and upset about many things" (see Lk. 10:41), that ancient prayer (*Lord Jesus Christ, Son of God, have mercy on me, a sinner*), when united to my breathing, has brought me to a place of quiet during many nights.

UNPLUG MACHINES. As an experiment in silence, try unplugging your life for an afternoon or for a day. Go around your house and turn off all the noisy machines, including cell phones, televisions, iPods, radios, computers, and every other electronic gadget that breaks the silence in your life. Then just sit in a room and soak in the silence as if in a hot tub. In our noisy, busy world, I've found great contentment in just sitting in a quiet place, enjoying the gift of silence and solitude, even if for only a few minutes each day. I especially soak in the silence on my weekly Sabbath day, which for me is on Friday. I take time to unplug my life and truly rest in the love of God through quiet time, reading, and walking in nature. A few years ago, MTV released a series of "unplugged" albums. The concept was to return to the simplicity of acoustic instruments, literally unplugging the electronic devices, including amplifiers, electric guitars, and digital keyboards. Unlike MTV, the movement to unplug our lives is no passing fad, but comes to us from the very heart of the Spirit of God, calling our spirits to come deeper, as the psalmist sings, "Deep calls to deep in the roar of your waterfalls" (Ps. 42:7a). Through regular times of silence and solitude, we discover a new attentiveness in our spirit, a fine-tuned ability to listen from the heart to the matters of the heart. One of the gifts of Benedictine formation is discovered in daily time of silence and solitude, time for us to rest our souls in God alone (see Ps. 62:1).

DEAL WITH DISTRACTIONS. Of course distractions and demands will continue to break into these brief interludes of grace. Like seniors making rounds in the monastery, we too need to assign "chaperones" to help us focus upon the gift of daily sacred reading of Scripture in silence and solitude. These chaperones might include a closed door, a muted cell phone, a "do not disturb" notice to other members of our family, or even asking a family member or friend to stand guard over our lives to keep us from wasting time or neglecting our reading.

THE PRACTICE OF *LECTIO DIVINA*

What is *lectio divina*? Literally, this Latin phrase can be translated as divine reading, or sacred reading. Practically, *lectio divina* combines reading and praying by inviting a reader to listen to the voice of the Lord as we draw near to Christ through slow, meditative reading of

Scripture. Though *lectio divina* is often thought of as a contemplative discipline, it is truly an evangelical practice. Through this practice, we center our lives upon Scripture and upon Christ, who is fully present through God's Word.

A few practical ideas may be helpful for entering into the daily habit of *lectio divina* within a local church. These are based upon Jesus' instructions on prayer to his followers: "When you pray, go into your room, close the door, and pray to your Father, who is unseen. Then your Father, who sees what is done in secret, will reward you" (Matt. 6:6). Here are the first three steps into this new way of studying Scripture.

GO INTO YOUR ROOM. First we must "go." We leave behind the ordinary duties and demands of daily life and remove our distractions in order to spend time in Scripture. This "going" involves moving into a new rhythm of life, by choosing a regular place, a nondrowsy time of the day, and a comfortable posture in which we can stay alert and attentive as we prepare to meet with God.

CLOSE THE DOOR. Second, we must "close the door." This act creates an enclosure, or a cloister, in which a person can enjoy unbroken time of intimacy with God. This act of closing the door includes removing interruptions, as well as creating a space that is conducive to personal time alone with God. This may mean lighting a candle, playing meditative music, and sitting in a comfortable, alert posture. We are also wise to have a good reading lamp, several books within easy reach (a Bible and other classic spiritual readings), a journal, and a pen. Each of these objects can help us in developing the sacred habit of *lectio divina*.

PRAY TO GOD. Third, we enter into personal time with God, who is unseen. Once we are seated in silence and solitude, we open a text of Scripture and begin our time of *lectio divina*—a discipline that has often been divided into four movements: reading, meditating, praying, and contemplating. Though these four movements are given in a specific order, the practice of daily *lectio divina* is a dynamic practice allowing a person to move back and forth between these four movements without being restricted to following the exact pattern as listed here. Historically, the four stages of *lectio divina* are traced to a twelfth-century treatise by Guigo II, *The Ladder of Monks and Twelve Meditations*, in which he describes these four movements as rungs on a ladder connecting earth to heaven. Here humans are united with God through contemplative discipline. As a practical way to enjoy fifteen minutes with the Lord and his Word, follow this guide into *lectio divina*.

READ. In the first movement, we read (Latin: *lectio*) the passage of Scripture, using our mind to observe the meaning of the text. The selection we choose may only be a paragraph or two. The pace of the reading is slower than normal reading as we pause upon a word or phrase to think about what is being read. Many people have found it helpful to quietly mouth the words aloud as they read, allowing their ears to hear the passage as their eyes see the passage. The purpose of this movement is to understand the text and the context in which these words are set. If the total time allotted is fifteen minutes, the first three or four minutes are for reading.

REFLECT. In the second movement, we reflect upon the passage aloud in order to mull over or meditate (Latin: *meditatio*) upon what we have read. During these five minutes, we think through the passage and recite aloud various words and phrases as we reflect inwardly upon the meaning of these words in relation to our life. We are mindful of God's presence, attentive to the Holy Spirit, listening for God's voice in the passage. We seek to meet Christ in the passage as we meditate on the Word, wrestling in our hearts with the intent and purpose of the passage for our growth in faith, hope, and love.

RESPOND. The third movement involves prayer (Latin: *oratio*). Once again, we read through the passage, but this time, we respond by allowing the words to carry us to God through verbal or mental prayer. We talk with God about the passage, asking questions, considering together with the Holy Spirit how the text could form our lives into the image of Christ. Allowing three or four minutes for this portion of *lectio divina*, we offer our spoken prayer to God, using the words and meanings of the passage to draw us into God's presence.

REST. The fourth movement of *lectio divina* invites us to contemplate (Latin: *contemplatio*), resting in God's heart through God's Word by surrendering our lives into God's care. We move past words, thoughts, and prayers and relax in God's presence, being alone with God in silence. This contemplation may last several minutes and can be closed with a quiet recitation of the Lord's Prayer to conclude the fifteen minutes of *lectio divina*.

Such an outline for this discipline may be practiced individually or in a small study group. For an excellent small group guide to *lectio divina*, see *Contemplative Bible Reading: Experiencing God Through Scripture* (Colorado Springs, CO: NavPress, 1999) by Richard Peace. In the past few years, Christians have begun to take more interest in this ancient approach to Scripture study, as evidenced by recent publications on *lectio divina* by such nationally known authors as Eugene H. Peterson, *Eat This Book: A Conversation in the Art of Spiritual Reading* (Grand Rapids, MI: Wm. B. Eerdmans, 2006); Richard J. Foster, *Life with God: Reading the Bible for Spiritual Transformation* (New York: HarperCollins, 2008); and Michael Casey,

OCSO, *Sacred Reading: The Ancient Art of* Lectio Divina (Liguori, MO: Triumph Books, 1996).

When practicing *lectio divina* in a group, we have the added potential for loving accountability—something Benedict values highly. Other people offer us encouragement as the members of a small group share their struggles to learn this new approach to an ancient practice. No new practice or habit comes easily. Benedict points out common problems of apathy, neglect, and distractions when we attempt something as basic as a daily time with God in the Scriptures. Other duties easily take precedent over this sacred task. We can spend long hours at computers or watching television programs, yet often find obstacles in the way of spending ten or fifteen minutes of time in the presence of God. In the past decade when I've introduced the Benedictine path of *lectio divina*, people have been hesitant at first to welcome something so different from well-known patterns of Bible study. Yet after a time, they have told me that *lectio divina* is like coming to a deep well of refreshing water where they truly quench their thirst for God.

SACRED SEASONS

One helpful way to develop the discipline of *lectio divina* is by observing the Christian year. New habits do not form overnight but rather through longer seasons. Though not every historic denomination celebrates the seasons of Advent and Lent, the days of Christmas and Easter are universally recognized by all followers of Jesus Christ as the great celebration days of the church year. In preparation for these holy days, we are wise to train our hearts during the weeks leading up to them. Historically, the church has set aside the four weeks prior to Christmas and the six weeks prior to Holy Week as seasons of special devotion and spiritual practices. Within these shorter seasons of Advent and Lent, *lectio divina* can take root in the daily practice of followers of the Lord who desire to grow through these seasons of spiritual expectancy.

In Advent (Latin, meaning *coming*), we not only prepare our lives for the celebration of Christ's birth, but we also prepare for the return of Christ in glory. During Lent (Old English for *springtime*), we recognize the forty days Jesus spent in the wilderness being tempted by Satan, as well as honoring other forty-day periods found throughout Scripture, in which great heroes of the faith encountered God through times of testing—Moses, Elijah, and Jonah. In the *Rule*, Benedict describes Lent as a season of self-denial and spiritual affirmation. "This we can do in a fitting manner by refusing to indulge evil habits and by devoting ourselves to prayer with tears, to reading, to compunction of heart and self-denial" (RB, 49.4).

The spiritual disciplines of self-denial include such acts as fasting from food or drink, denying some pleasure, removing bad habits. The Christ-affirming disciplines include prayers, *lectio divina*, and giving service to others in need. Above all, Benedict calls us to do all "*with the joy of the Holy Spirit* (1 Thess. 1:6)," and to "look forward to holy Easter with joy and spiritual longing" (RB, 49.6–7). As a Benedictine Oblate, I receive a "Bona Opera" (good work) card every year at the beginning of the season of Lent. On this card, Oblates write down their Lenten plan of devotion and return these cards for the blessing of the abbot. As we enter into new practices of faith, we are wise to bring them before a friend or spiritual director for their affirmation and encouragement and ask for support in prayer as we prepare to enter upon these seasons of growth (see RB, 49.9).

Finally, we need to ask what we can carry home with us from the treasures we have received from *lectio divina*. Like children on Christmas day, we find great joy unwrapping the treasures of books, silence, solitude, *lectio divina*, and the celebration of holy seasons along the journey through the year. The following suggestions offer guidance for growth in Christ:

COMMIT TO BECOMING A LIFELONG LEARNER. Wherever we travel, we can always bring along a book, especially the Bible. Read the great works of the saints of old. Every year, befriend one of the great heroes of the faith, and walk alongside him or her for months until you really begin to understand the way he or she lived, what he or she wrote, and how he or she practiced Christian formation.

LEARN TO PRACTICE THE ART OF *LECTIO DIVINA*. Approaching Scripture through reading, reflecting, responding, and resting has been one of the most transformative gifts of grace from the ancient church to our current age. The sacred art of *lectio divina*, practiced for centuries, has once again found fertile soil in the hearts of millions of people—hearts where God's Word will bear fruit that will last into eternity.

BRING THESE SPIRITUAL HABITS ALONG WITH YOU IN YOUR LIFE JOURNEY. There are many others in the local church, in your family, and among your circle of friends who will likely benefit from such a refreshing approach to life with God as *lectio divina*. As Benedict wisely advises, "Those who have been sent on a journey are not to omit the prescribed hours but to observe them as best they can, not neglecting their measure of service" (RB, 50.4). Christian formation is not just for those times when we are in a stable, steady rhythm of life. These practices are to be carried with us throughout our daily life. All of our life may be viewed as a holy pilgrimage in which we "are to perform the Work of God where [we] are . . . out of reverence for God" (RB, 50.3). The first four Benedictine paths of Christian formation, including Prayer, Spiritual Guidance, Ordinary Spirituality, and *Lectio Divina*, would be impossible to practice without life in the final village of hospitality, where pilgrims are invited to come in out of the weather, to rest and refresh themselves within a warm and loving home of Christian hospitality.

TAKING STEPS
INTO CHRISTIAN FORMATION
from Chapter Six

- Consider turning off your computer, cell phone, electronic games, CD players, iPods, and any other electronic gadget. Then, open the pages of the Bible. Commit yourself to reading from the Bible ten or fifteen minutes every day. Ask a friend to hold you accountable to this new pattern.

- Obtain books from a series of classic Christian spiritual writings and enjoy listening to wisdom from the past.

- Elect to spend time in silence and in solitude every week or every month for a year. See how these spiritual disciplines influence your use of words and your time spent with others.

- Learn to practice *lectio divina* following the guidelines from chapter six. Read, reflect upon, respond to, and rest in God's Word. Once you've begun to learn this pattern, share it with a few others, and practice *lectio divina* with fellow pilgrims of faith.

- Celebrate the sacred seasons of the church year with friends. Invite a group of fellow believers to commit to joining together each season for a whole year, beginning during Advent. Share together creative ways to enter more fully into the birth, life, death, and resurrection of our Lord Jesus Christ. Celebrate together the lives of the saints of God who have walked this pilgrim path before us.

CHAPTER 7

The Path of Hospitality

Nearly 100,000 people make the annual five-hundred-mile pilgrimage known as *Camino de Santiago* to the city of Santiago in northern Spain. The pilgrims average around fifteen miles per day on foot, walking a full month along the pilgrim route, stopping off at pilgrim hostels each night for food and lodging. Such a challenging pilgrimage would be impossible without pilgrim hostels where travelers are welcomed, provided a place to share a meal, bathe, and rest a while, before pressing on in their journey.

Like the pilgrims on the *Camino de Santiago*, we need "hostels" on our life journey where we are welcomed and offered the gift of hospitality. Our fifth path of Christian formation is the Benedictine practice of hospitality. In this chapter, we will explore how to welcome strangers, receive and care for guests in practical ways, and encourage creativity in our practice of hospitality, and we will take longer strides into world-changing hospitality.

WELCOMED AS CHRIST

One of the most revolutionary sentences I've ever read in classic Christian writings may be found in chapter 53 of *The Rule of St. Benedict*: "All guests who present themselves are to be welcomed as Christ, for he himself will say: *I was a stranger and you welcomed me* (Matt. 25:35)" (RB, 53.1). When I am busy with many other activities, I've found it is very easy to overlook the strangers around me. We often pass by strangers without giving them any form of recognition or greeting. Benedictine hospitality invites us to consider these people in a radically new way. We are looking into the face of Christ when we look into the eyes of a stranger. How many opportunities do we miss to spend time with Christ through the life of a stranger each day? The *Rule* revolutionized the Western world's approach to strangers. This way of hospitality encourages an openhearted, adventurous approach to all strangers, especially fellow believers, the poor, and pilgrims: three classes of people specially honored by Benedict.

This approach to strangers is even more amazing when we understand the times in which Benedict lived. During his lifetime, the Roman Empire was in a state of decline and turmoil. Barbarian tribes, including the Goths and the Vandals, attacked down the spine of Italy with increasing frequency, leaving people in constant fear of invasion, famine, and disease. Benedict lived in a time of widespread societal distress and upheaval, and yet, he still called his monks to take the risk of welcoming the stranger "as Christ."

True hospitality requires risk taking—walking the Emmaus Road with the stranger who is Christ (see Lk. 24:13–35). Here are four practical ways to carry out this understanding of hospitality along the "Emmaus Road."

- Take time during your day to talk with someone you've never met. Listen to their stories and share in their lives.
- Welcome a pilgrim traveler to spend the night in your home.
- Sit at a table and break bread with a hungry person.

- Go out of your way to befriend the lonely and invite them into your life.

When we accept the holy calling of hospitality, Christ is revealed to our eyes, to our families, and to our world. As we open the simple gifts of Benedictine spirituality, including the gift of hospitality, we receive God's grace of a deeper, more joyful life together in Christ. The practice of hospitality calls us to step outside our comfort zone into the lives of those we meet. We can look into the face of a stranger and see the eyes of Christ looking back.

Allow me an example or two from my life in Cannon Beach. Our town is a popular beach resort and artist colony that attracts hundreds of thousands of out-of-town guests every year. The year-round residential population of Cannon Beach is around 2,000 people. We have ten miles of pristine beaches, with some of the most beautiful coastal scenery in the world. We also have twenty-five art galleries. During the summer months, thousands of people come to town daily to walk the beaches, visit the art galleries, and enjoy the cozy, quaint beach town we call home. By August, local citizens start to grumble about all the visitors. I too get frustrated at times trying to find a parking space downtown in the summer, or getting stuck behind bumper-to-bumper traffic when I'm late to a meeting. Chapter 53 of the *Rule* has helped me to see every guest who comes to Cannon Beach "as Christ," for it is Christ hidden in the person of this stranger whom I greet.

The same challenges face the people of Community Presbyterian Church. Every Sunday, month after month, about one-third of the people attending worship are from out of town. How easy it is to overlook these guests and only visit with our familiar church friends rather than reaching out to strangers. Benedict keeps challenging us to welcome Christ in our midst, to get to know the stranger by welcoming them as family into God's house.

One more way Benedict's vision of hospitality has guided us as a people involves how we treat others when there is conflict. Every healthy relationship experiences conflict and tension at times. When the other person is viewed "as Christ," whether in the marriage relationship, or among friends, or between members of a church family, there is a quicker movement between people to seek forgiveness and offer hospitality.

This Christ-centered approach to hospitality calls us to look at people with new eyes. As Paul wrote, "So from now on we regard no one from a worldly point of view. Though we once regarded Christ in this way, we do so no longer. Therefore, if anyone is in Christ, he is a new creation; the old has gone, the new has come" (2 Cor. 5:16–17). Christian hospitality invites us to look at people, no longer from a worldly point of view but as in Christ. This new way of looking at people is a habit of the heart that can be developed through the intentional choices we make daily when spending time with others.

The gift of hospitality also includes such practical acts as providing food, drink, music, and lodging for people who at first are strangers and guests. An ancient Celtic poem, the "Celtic Rune of Hospitality," speaks of this vision of hospitality:

> I saw a stranger today.
> I put food for him in the eating-place
> And drink in the drinking-place
> And music in the listening-place.
> In the Holy name of the Trinity
> He blessed myself and my family.

And the lark said in her warble
Often, often, often
Goes Christ in the stranger's guise.
O, oft and oft and oft,
Goes Christ in the stranger's guise.

As we welcome people into our lives "as Christ," we begin to treat them as friends and members of the family, overlooking their shortcomings, willingly providing for their needs, and eagerly sharing life together in Christ. Recently, we welcomed a stranger into our home, a woman who was bicycling around the world. A friend of a friend passed along her name to us, saying she likely would be coming through town in a few days. We got in touch with this bicyclist pilgrim and welcomed her into our home for a few nights. She left her native land of Great Britain, headed east across Europe and Asia, and arrived on the north coast of Oregon after nearly two years of travels. Though we had never met before, we welcomed her as a member of our family, and discovered she shared our love for Christ. We enjoyed two days of stories, meals, prayers, and blessings with her before sending her on her way, across America.

Opportunities present themselves daily to meet Christ in the face of our children, spouse, neighbor, or guest, and to welcome these people with love. We offer hospitality by inviting them to join us in our journey, to come into our home, share a common meal, and find rest for their lives. As we welcome people, our eyes keep opening to the glory of Christ in our midst, and we discover that our hearts are "burning within us" (see Lk. 24:32), knowing that we've once again spent time with Christ along the way.

HOSPITALITY AS MENTORING

Benedict provides detailed instructions regarding developing a ministry of hospitality, and puts an emphasis upon personal mentoring. First, we are to meet a guest "with all the courtesy of love" (RB, 53.3), and we are to "pray together and thus be united in peace" (RB, 53.4). We welcome a guest into our lives with "all humility," both in their arrival and departure, for "Christ is to be adored because he is indeed welcomed in them" (RB, 53.6–7). While a guest is present in our life, "every kindness is shown to him" (RB, 53.9), including such acts of kindness as opportunities to wash, eat, rest, sleep, and renew their lives while in our care.

Within a busy local church, we are called by God to welcome guests as Christ. Practically speaking, this means mentoring people, including learning their names, sharing life stories, taking time to get to know guests as if they are members of our own family, as well as encouraging them in their journey of faith. In a larger church, or in a congregation such as Community Presbyterian Church that sees many guests every week, this ministry of hospitality as mentoring needs to be carefully orchestrated with trained volunteers providing a warm personal greeting, as well as regular encouragement to members to see the face of Christ in the face of a stranger. One of the greatest obstacles to growth in a local church is simply the number of people attending. The larger the local church, the less people know about one another. Often, church members have no idea who is a first-time guest and who has been a member for several decades. Here are a few ideas that will help people get to know one another better, and help make guests feel more like part of the family:

WELCOMING GUESTS AS FAMILY

- Develop a list of greeters who will become the "face" of the church family to every person coming into the church. Train these people to meet guests face-to-face, to welcome them warmly, to learn their names, and to call them by name week by week.

- Recruit informal sanctuary hosts who oversee an area of the sanctuary, perhaps twenty or thirty seats, and who get to know each person sitting in that area—people tend to sit in the same area week after week. Have these hosts track the new arrivals, as well as those who have been absent for a few weeks.

- Employ name cards for regular church family members, and encourage everyone to wear name cards to improve face to name recognition. Invite guests to wear a name card that is available at a welcome center in the church foyer.

- Warmly welcome guests each week from the pulpit, and publicly make them feel part of the family.

- Consider creating a new photo directory of the church family every few years to assist new people to put names with faces. Put one of these photo directories in the church foyer for reference.

- Invite newcomers to attend a welcome lunch or dessert where they can informally learn about the church family, meet a few leaders, including a pastor, elder, and church member, as well as ask any questions they may have about the life of the church.

- Assign mentors to every new member who joins the church, and encourage new members and their mentors to meet informally on a monthly basis during the first year of membership.

In the *Rule* Benedict offers us specific guidelines for receiving members into the family of faith in a way that encourages their Christian formation. The long-term ministry of hospitality in the life of a church involves assimilating new people into the life of the congregation. The *Rule* encourages mentoring new members in the community. A "senior chosen for his skill in winning souls should be appointed to look after [newcomers] with careful attention" (RB, 58.6). This mentor is encouraged to discern whether a newcomer "truly seeks God and whether he shows eagerness for the Work of God" (RB, 58.7).

Mentoring includes studying Scripture and offering basic instructions in the faith and in the mission of the congregation. People want to know what kind of community they are joining. What is the purpose and mission of this family of faith? How can we get involved? Where can we find a place to serve? What local charities do you support? What missionaries are you supporting? Who are your leaders? How are they chosen? Where can I find a Bible study or prayer group to join? How might our experiences and spiritual gifts be put to use here? These are the kinds of questions people often ask as they begin to step into the life of the congregation. Through the gift of mentoring, people discover the answer to such questions, as the relationship with their mentor unfolds over weeks and months. Of course, mentoring is more than merely answering questions; it is developing a friendship that helps the guest become a valued member of the family of faith.

The *Rule* offers a new approach to accepting new members—an approach that most congregations today may have never considered. Benedict encourages the members of a community of faith to take their time, allowing months of formation with a newcomer to unfold before officially welcoming them into active membership in the community. During these months of formation, the *Rule* is read aloud to a newcomer three times—after two months, six months, and ten months. "Let him be told: 'This is the law under which you are choosing to serve. If you can keep it, come in. If not, feel free to leave'" (RB, 58.10).

The principle expressed in this writing is hospitality through mentoring. Benedictine spirituality involves intentional, long-term mentoring of guests who come into the house of faith, and inviting newcomers into the community along the paths of Christian formation.

In our contemporary, busy culture, Benedict's slow, intentional approach to spiritual growth offers a radical alternative to our high-speed expectations for success. Benedict boldly asserts that there is no such thing as instant Christian formation. The life of Christ is formed in a person over months and years, through mentoring within a faith community, involving hundreds of hours of care and accountability. Pastors and elders within local congregations are wise to develop a variety of tools that will help new members and mentors grow through these months of Christian formation. Such tools may include spiritual gift assessment inventories, leadership training tools, Scripture memory, Bible study methods, as well as a spiritual formation training curriculum for developing such habits as praying the Psalms and *lectio divina.*

In addition to preparing new members for lifelong involvement within the local congregation, the ministry of hospitality as mentoring also involves the preparation and training of church members for lifelong service in ministry. Everyone has an active role of Christian service to offer as part of the local body of Christ. One of the key tasks of lay leaders within a local church is helping people discover their unique giftedness, gain confidence to put their gifts into practice, and implement these gifts in service for the Lord.

In addition to volunteer service, many churches have paid internship ministries in which they hire "ministers in training," Bible school students, or seminarians to spend a season or a year with the congregation in order to learn by doing. With proper supervision and mentoring, such internships offer a win-win relationship between a congregation and an intern. The intern gains from the shared wisdom the congregation imparts through investing in the life of the intern. The congregation gains from the new vitality and vision the intern brings into the life of the church. In 2009, the congregation where I serve as pastor welcomed a young Bible school student from Malawi, Africa, who came for a summer internship. Our summer together with this young African intern deeply moved many people and stretched their horizons while it deepened our shared life in Christ. What a gift to join with our family of faith in Africa! Though these seasons are brief, they can leave a lasting positive impact upon both the host church and the resident intern.

WELCOMING CREATIVITY

Throughout history, the church has provided a welcome place for artists. God's people have been inspired by the Holy Spirit to encourage creative people to practice their God-given talent in creating pieces of beauty as an expression of devotion. Along with many church leaders before him, Benedict welcomed creativity as a daily form of Christian formation. "If there are artisans in the monastery, they are to practice their craft with all humility . . . *so that in all things God may be glorified* (1 Pet. 4:11)" (RB, 57.1, 9).

By affirming the arts, Benedict contributed to the rise of the artisan middle class in Europe. This included the development of artisan skills in woodworking, manuscript reproduction, barrel making, winemaking, leather craft, blacksmith work, pottery, and many other handcrafts. As these crafts developed within the stability of the cloister, local artisan guilds sprang up, with apprenticeships from local villages sending novice workers to study under master craftsmen in the monasteries. Such apprenticeships still exist, but seldom are they connected to local congregations. Mostly, they are found within the world of professional art, which includes musicians, painters, and potters, as well as within the world of skilled tradesmen such as plumbers and electricians. Yet, the practice of teaching an artistic skill to a younger student is a valuable practice even among amateurs, as it becomes one more link to connect people. Connected to these informal art lessons are lessons in spiritual formation as we share our lives together. Other such apprenticeships might include writing, drama, dance, or painting workshops where artists meet together to review each other's creative works and offer constructive critique. In recent years, seminaries have added formal studies in theology and the arts.

One example is the Brehm Center for the Arts at Fuller Theological Seminary, which offers degrees in art and theology with special emphases on filmmaking, visual arts, architecture, music, and preaching. In all these approaches to creativity, we practice hospitality in the name of Christ, for "all things were created by him and for him . . . and in him all things hold together" (Col. 1:16c–17). The greatest work of art in a local church never hangs on a wall nor is it written in a songbook, but it is discovered in the person sitting next to you. God's ongoing creation and artistic handiwork is the work of art unfolding in the lives of the followers of Christ. "For we are God's workmanship, created in Christ Jesus to do good works, which God prepared in advance for us to do" (Eph. 2:10).

WORLD-CHANGING HOSPITALITY

The God of all creation invites us to reach out to this world with hospitable hearts, welcoming the poor, the stranger, the homeless, the sick, and the outcast in Jesus' name. For some, the immensity of the task of caring for needy people in this world is overwhelming. I often feel overwhelmed by the challenges facing millions of people around the world, and feel guilty for not doing more for these people. I've been richly blessed in the past two decades to be part of a generous, globally minded congregation—a group of people who love to give away nearly a quarter of the weekly offering to help others in need. More than merely giving money, globally minded pilgrims also invest their hearts and lives in reaching out to the world with the love of Christ through prayers, letters, mission projects, and intentional world travel, or short-term mission trips. We've seen more than a dozen members of our local church go out on short-term mission trips over the past few years to such countries as Costa Rica, China, Malawi, Ukraine, Macedonia, Cambodia, Germany, Russia, and South Africa. On each of these mission trips, people were transformed by their time away and challenged us upon their return with a sense of adventure and openhearted welcome to the needy people of the world.

Monastic life is often misrepresented as avoiding the needs of the world. People look at the isolation of the monastic community in rural areas within the confining walls of the cloister and assume monks care little for the needy of the world. Nothing could be further from the truth of Benedictine spirituality. The intentional life of the community requires every monk to actively engage in world-changing hospitality through daily work and prayer. As monks lay down their lives within the community, they offer themselves as living sacrifices for the sake of the needy of this world. They sacrifice wealth, private property, and personal freedom so that they can dedicate their lives to prayer and caring for others through hospitality and service.

Benedict's vision of hospitality is a radical call to transform society, person by person, through spiritual and physical means, as it seeks to welcome Christ through the stranger, the sick, the homeless, and the poor by working to provide for the needy in the community and praying for the needy around the world. The fact that two million people die every year of HIV/AIDS in Africa can easily overwhelm even the most visionary idealists among us. Who is going to begin to help love all those millions of orphans bereft of their parents?

Benedictine spirituality calls us to step out of our comfort zone and creatively make a difference in this world. In declaring hospitality an essential part of Christian formation, Benedict was not creating a new movement, but rather fulfilling the call of Scripture. "Religion that God our Father accepts as pure and faultless is this: to look after orphans and widows in their distress and to keep oneself from being polluted by the world" (Jas. 1:27). This approach to the spiritual life, which requires both lifestyle purity and "radical hospitality," is part of the genius of Benedictine spirituality as it has been practiced for centuries.

"How does one person with great talents come to exert a force on the world?" Tracy Kidder asks this profound question toward the end of his best-selling book, *Mountains Beyond Mountains: The Quest of Dr. Paul Farmer, a Man Who Would Cure the World*. Kidder tells the story of Dr. Paul Farmer, a physician who believes he can eradicate tuberculosis from the face of this planet. The price tag he offers is five billion dollars. Tuberculosis is one of the three most destructive worldwide pandemics, along with HIV/AIDS and malaria. Can we truly make a difference in this world for good? Is there a cure for millions of people who are dying of one of these three killers? Who will step into the lives of "the least of these brothers of mine" (see Matt. 25:40) to offer a cup of cold water, housing, medical care, and a compassionate heart? How can we practice world-changing hospitality? Each of us, in our own way, is invited by God to share in this adventure by laying down our lives for the sake of others, by recognizing the unseen presence of Christ in the face of the stranger, and by discovering that we too have "great talents," that we can "exert a force on the world" for good.

Dr. Farmer discovered how to go about changing his world after meeting a nun who was giving her life away to help the poor. He was in college at the time.

> Here I am in the middle of a very affluent university, with a lot of comfortable ideas, and I met this nun. She was Belgian, Juliana DeWolf, working with the Friends of the United Farm Workers. And she was a fearless article. I just remember thinking she was much more radical and committed than anyone I'd met, arrogant and humble at the same time. The Haitian farm workers thought the world of her.

He decided his life purpose was to be a medical doctor to the poorest of the poor in Haiti, seeking to cure the worst diseases on the planet. He has invested his life over the past thirty years among the poor in Haiti, seeking to wipe out tuberculosis in the central plain of that troubled country. By seeking to fulfill one of the great cries of faith from the prophet Micah, "To act justly, and to love mercy, and to walk humbly with your God" (6:8), Dr. Paul Farmer shows in his life what a difference one person can make upon the world for good.

Allow me an example of world-changing hospitality a little closer to home. In 1989, I was serving as campus pastor at Middle Tennessee State University. One day, the international student director on campus called me with a need. An African international student had arrived that day, only to discover his government's promise to fund his education had changed overnight. While he was in flight over the Atlantic, his government underwent a military coup, freezing all foreign assets going out of the country. We discussed possible options for this penniless African guest. After spending his first few days in our home, we found a more permanent housing arrangement for our new African friend. He was welcomed into the home of a retired college history professor. The professor and his wife lived alone and needed someone to look after the house while they visited their grandchildren in a neighboring state. This white Christian couple agreed to welcome a black African Muslim into their home for a little while to see how it might work out. There was no political agenda in the arrangement: it was just the civility of Christ-centered hospitality that welcomed a stranger into their home. The housing arrangement lasted over four years, until the student from Africa graduated from the university, met his wife, and moved into his own home. Afterward, the professor and his wife told me that the arrival of their Muslim friend was one of the best gifts God had ever brought them.

This particular way of hospitality may not be for everyone, but it offers a creative way to engage a needy world and embrace the person of Christ through the stranger at our door. Other approaches to world-changing hospitality may include learning a foreign language through a weekly tutorial with a person from another country, opening our home to traveling artists, becoming foster parents to neglected kids, or legally adopting an orphan. Such forms of world-changing hospitality will have the greatest impact when they involve a community working together. Margaret Mead (1901–78), an anthropologist known for her work on the relationship of culture and personality, was known to have claimed the following: "Never doubt that a small group of thoughtful, committed citizens can change the world. Indeed, it is the only thing that ever has."

Christian formation calls us into such an intentional world-changing community. At its heart, the church is a "small group of thoughtful, committed" citizens of Christ who have the heart conviction that we can transform the world for good, person by person. "Unless a kernel of wheat falls to the ground and dies, it remains only a single seed. But if it dies, it produces many seeds" (Jn. 12:24). Benedict shows us that world-changing hospitality begins and ends with the love of Christ. We are brought out of a life of self-centeredness and sent into our needy world, both through the love of Christ. Only by living a life centered upon Christ will we have the energy and love to truly make a difference in this world for good. As Benedict writes near the end of the *Rule*, "Let them prefer nothing whatever to Christ, and may he bring us all together to everlasting life" (RB, 72.1–12).

TAKING STEPS
INTO CHRISTIAN FORMATION
from Chapter Seven

- Walk the Emmaus Road with Christ by taking time in your day to talk with a stranger, to welcome a pilgrim into your home, to sit at a table and share food with a hungry person, or to go out of your way to befriend a lonely person.

- Commit yourself to reach out to guests every week before and after worship and help to make people feel welcome at worship. Learn their names. Ask questions about their lives. Invite them to come to your home for a meal. Consider volunteering as a greeter or part of the hospitality team in your local church. Take an active interest in spending time with people, learning their names, sharing life stories, treating everyone as part of your family.

- Encourage artists you know by providing space for them to create their art if that is needed, or by arranging for commissions for their artwork. If you are part of a leadership team in a local church, consider allowing local artists to utilize space within the church building for a studio.

- Invite international students over for a meal in your home, or invite them as guests to live in your home for a season.

- Consider making a sacred pilgrimage, such as the *Camino de Santiago*. While you are on this pilgrimage, pay attention to patterns of hospitality offered to you as a pilgrim. Write in a journal some new insights on offering hospitality to pilgrims.

- Welcome strangers "as Christ." Look at all people as though they are Christ here in your midst. Reflect upon how this way of looking at other people changes your way of thinking about strangers, guests, visitors, and foreigners.

- Make a difference in this world by creatively reaching out to needy people through the practice of world-changing hospitality in the lives of refugees, orphans, widows, hungry people, the homeless, war victims, and other hurting people all around the world.

PART TWO

CHRISTIAN FORMATION AS A WAY OF LIFE TOGETHER

CHAPTER 8

How Benedict Is Still Transforming the World

Before they step out into the unknown wilderness, hikers usually study maps and trail guidebooks to better understand what lies ahead. Without such guidance, hikers run the risk of losing their way. In a similar manner, the *Rule* may be considered an expert trail guidebook for the journey of Christian formation. Benedict believed we are to make this journey with others, guided by lifelong commitments, or vows, and also by a *rule of life*. In the following chapter, we will stand once again at the trailhead to study how Benedict is still transforming the world through three life commitments of Christian formation—the vows of stability, fidelity, and obedience.

THE VOW OF STABILITY IN COMMUNITY

Benedict grew up in the late fifth-century Italy, a time marked by widespread unrest and instability. Early in his life, Benedict personally experienced some of this instability—leaving home as a teenager to begin formal studies in Rome; and then after a brief time in Rome, abandoning the city, traveling into the mountains to the east of Rome to seek a deeper life with God. His first three years as a monk were lived in solitude in a cave. He seldom left the stone walls of this cell, but stayed in his cave, day and night, to devote his life to prayer. He moved once again, leaving his life of solitude in the cave to join with a local band of monks as their spiritual father. After a few years of stability near Subiaco, he moved again, traveling south to the hilltop location of Monte Cassino. From these humble beginnings, it comes as no big surprise that Benedict introduced a vow of stability for all monks who desired to lay down their lives for Christ. The vow of stability stands as one of the great gifts Benedict has given to the world of spiritual formation. This vow offers our world today a powerful antidote to excessive mobility and contemporary forms of instability. Many people today lack roots, and are often on the move to the next job, the next relationship, and the next house in the next city.

A lack of roots was a concern of the early Christian writers, including the Desert Fathers several centuries prior to Benedict, as evidenced in the desert instruction, "just as a tree cannot bear fruit if it is often transplanted, so neither can a monk bear fruit if he frequently changes his abode." As gardeners know, plants require healthy root systems to grow to full maturity. Uprooting a plant too often stresses the health of the plant and limits the potential for growth and fruitfulness. When Benedict called monks to a vow of stability, he understood such a life-commitment would plant an individual monk into the root system of the monastic community where he would mature in faith, hope, and love. In Benedict's understanding, stability is more about community than geography, more about a commitment to people than to a place.

How might this relate to those of us who are not monks? Consider with me how views have changed in the past century of community life in America. In the early twentieth century, American life was shaped largely by farming communities; most of the population lived in rural America. In just one hundred years, our way of life has been dramatically transformed by the invention of the automobile and by mass migrations to the cities of America. According to the U.S. Census, in 1890 nearly 70 percent of Americans lived in rural America. A century later in 1990, 75 percent of the population lived in cities. The percentage of the American farm labor force dramatically dropped from 40 percent in 1890 to 2 percent in 1990.

The invention of the automobile and the airplane increased the distance and frequency of travel for Americans and revolutionized the way humans viewed their local community. The first patent for a motor car was from Karl Benz of Germany in 1886. Less than twenty years later in 1903, the Wright brothers made their historic flight at Kitty Hawk. By the mid-twentieth century, instead of walking to the nearest church or school, people began to drive across town to attend church or school. Instead of taking a horse-drawn cart to market to do business, by the 1950s, people began to board airplanes to fly to distant cities to do business. Whereas church buildings of rural America in the nineteenth century were surrounded by graveyards, church buildings built in America since World War II were surrounded by parking lots. The automobile fit right into American cultural values of individualism and privatization—values that have also influenced the life of the local church. I'm not saying churches need to do away with their parking lots. The automobile is here to stay, and churches are wise to provide adequate parking as a way of welcoming people into the community of faith. But looking back over the past century, we can see how fast our way of life has changed—a dramatic move away from stability in community.

Besides the automobile, other forms of technology have also eroded the stability of life together in community, especially within the community of faith. One of the most powerful change-agents in the twentieth century was television, which brought the world into our living rooms. This included Christian programming. Individuals and families were offered new opportunities to worship via television. Worship services featuring celebrity preachers and televangelists were beamed into the living room via satellite dish. Since the advent of the Internet, the local church community has become more and more marginalized for many former worshipers. Without a commitment to remain rooted in the community, an individual could easily get out of the habit of attending weekly worship with a group of fellow believers in Christ. The rise of the cyber-church or e-congregation of the future will continue to offer greater numbers of people an alternative to "going to church"—by the simple click of a button on a personal computer, laptop, or iPhone.

What would it mean for us to live according to a vow of stability in a community within this mobile society? Is it reasonable to ask people to commit to such a vow? How might such a vow of stability help people in our world today? Consider with me several places in society where such commitments of stability are already in place, offering people protection and support for growth.

Marriage vows are essentially a lifelong commitment to stability within a community of a husband and a wife. Married life together presents challenges even to the healthiest of couples. Without vows, many couples simple drift away from each other and look for someone who will better meet their needs. Within marriage vows, couples have a lifelong foundation upon which to work out their conflicts and grow together in their shared life.

Think also of two other arenas of valued stability—public office and business. Elected officials are sworn into office in a public ceremony in which the newly elected officer agrees to an oath of service. Several years ago, I was elected to serve on our local school board. Along with all other public officials, I solemnly took an oath of office; a vow of stability in community.

In the world of business, employers also ask employees for commitments—a commitment to the mission of the corporation, and often a commitment to work for the company for a set period of time. These could be viewed as vows of stability, because they offer the company the protection and support needed to conduct its business. As we look at each of these settings—marriage, community service, and business—we may find encouragement for a local church to introduce a vow of stability for new members.

Some of the instability facing the local congregation may also be found among professional clergy. Ministers can be influenced by cultural forms of instability and seek to climb the ecclesiastical ladder of success, moving from smaller church settings to multistaff pastoral positions to the ultimate goal of becoming head of staff at a large church. This movement tends to lead pastors from rural to suburban or urban settings. According to the Barna Research Group, pastors move on an average of every six years. As George Barna noted in 2001,

> Our work has found that the typical pastor has his or her greatest ministry impact at a church in years five through fourteen of their pastorate. Unfortunately, we also know that the average pastor lasts only five years at a church—forfeiting the fruit of their investment in the church they've pastored. In our fast turnaround society where we demand overnight results and consider everyone expendable and everything disposable, we may be shortchanging pastors—and the congregations they oversee—by prematurely terminating their tenure.

The Benedictine vow of stability offers a healthy alternative to a contemporary culture seduced by a ladder-climbing approach to career development. Often, when people ask me how long I plan on staying in Cannon Beach, I tell them "as long as the Lord allows!" I also tell people that I've taken a vow of stability, and will remain planted here as long as my life bears good fruit in this community. Such a vow can help both clergy and congregations to work through difficulties as they have mutually committed to long-term faithfulness through stability in community. As Joan Chittister, OSB, writes,

> Benedictine stability is a promise to meet life head-on. . . . Stability teaches that whatever the depth of the dullness or the difficulties around me, I can, if I will simply stay still enough of heart, find God there in the midst of them. . . . What enables a person to keep going back to the difficult parts of life is, inevitably, certitude in the faithfulness of God.

Stability does not rest upon mere human effort, but is rooted in the faithfulness of God and the love of Christ, who invited his followers to a life of stability. "Remain in me, and I will remain in you. No branch can bear fruit by itself; it must remain in the vine. Neither can you bear fruit unless you remain in me" (Jn. 15:4). The Greek verb Jesus used in this statement, *meinate*, connotes an intimate connection, such as a branch that is attached to the trunk of a vine. Through a life of stability, we connect our lives to Christ in an intimate relationship, rooted in the faithfulness of God. Like a branch attached in stability to the vine, we discover fruit growing in our life as the grace of Jesus Christ flows like sap into us, especially through the life of the faith community.

The vow of stability keeps a local church growing together in Christ rather than avoiding the hard work of sharing life in community. The good work of Christian formation takes years of daily living within the stability of a community of believers who allow the grace of God to shape their lives day by day. Inherent in this life of stability is a strange paradox involving two conflicting metaphors: standing still and journeying. We move forward in faith by standing still in the faithfulness of God. We dynamically grow up into Christian maturity by rooting ourselves deeply in the grace of Jesus Christ. Gregory of Nyssa clearly understood this view of Christian growth:

> This is the most marvelous thing of all: how the same thing is both a standing still and a moving. . . . I mean by this that the firmer and the more immovable one remains in the Good, the more he progresses in the course of virtues. . . . It is like using the standing still as if it were a wing while the heart flies upward through its stability in the Good.

Taking a vow of stability does not preclude moving from place to place. It is more of an attitude that says, "I will not run away when difficult choices or situations arise." Stability as a way of life commits us to being together with fellow pilgrims with whom we intend to worship, live, and grow in our shared life in Christ. Thus, no matter where we move or how often we move, followers of Christ seek stability within a community of faith where we can plant our roots and grow in love.

THE VOW OF FIDELITY IN COMMUNITY

The second Benedictine vow, in Latin *conversatio morum*, does not have a natural English equivalent, but is commonly translated as either "conversion of life" or "fidelity to the monastic way of life." This second vow expresses our openness to be converted by Christ within a community of believers over a lifetime. As Esther de Waal describes this vow,

> To say that I will journey on, whatever the cost and wherever that may lead me, is not to say that I believe I can do this through my own strength of will or strong sense of moral purpose. It shows my utter reliance on God. . . . Essentially, this is the interior journey, a journey inward, and its goal is conversion of heart. When do we arrive? There is no stopping place in this life no matter how far along the road we may have come.

According to M. Basil Pennington, ocso, this second Benedictine vow involves "a continual transformation of the mind and heart according to God's plan for us." The second vow offers an alternative to the private lifestyle of the hermit mentioned by Benedict in the first chapter of the *Rule*. It also provides an antidote to self-centered living. As Pennington asserts,

> This vow of the common, cenobitic way of life is contrary to the singularity of the eremitic or anchorite life. . . . It is a challenge for all of us to constantly watch ourselves for tendencies to singularity, self-will, and instability.

Instead of living as independent, self-willed islands, we are joined to the mainland of the Christian community. As Thomas Merton wrote in *No Man Is an Island*,

> Every other man is a piece of myself, for I am a part and a member of mankind. Every Christian is part of my own body, because we are members of Christ. What I do is also done for them and with them and by them. . . . Nothing at all makes sense, unless we admit, with John Donne, that: "No man is an island, entire of itself; every man is a piece of the continent, a part of the main."

Merton's final lecture, delivered just hours before he died in Bangkok, Thailand, on December 10, 1968, was addressed to an international community of monks from a variety of religious faith traditions. In this speech, Merton spoke of the second Benedictine vow as "the most essential."

> When you stop and think a little about St. Benedict's concept of *conversatio morum*, that most mysterious of our vows, which is actually the most essential, I believe, it can be interpreted as a commitment to total inner transformation of one sort or another—a commitment to become completely a new man. It seems to me that that could be regarded as the end of the monastic life, and that no matter where one attempts to do this, that remains the essential thing.

The essential nature of the second vow lies in the twofold promise to conversion of life through both the intentional connection to Christ and through the personal connection to the community of Christ. In Terrence Kardong's words, "the ancients assumed that acceptance of the monastic lifestyle would imply a thorough change of the person on a deep level." The process of spiritual formation in an individual occurs through living in loving accountability within a local faith community that is connected to the universal body of Christ. Whether we acknowledge it or not, we are all part of a global community of faith—the universal Church. We find lasting growth together, not apart. Most of us need the support and loving accountability of the faith community to remain faithful to our calling in Christ. Most of us will only continue to be spiritually formed throughout our lives if we remain faithful to a local faith community. Benedictine spirituality is filled with theological paradoxes, including such creative tensions as found between these first two vows. Change comes from remaining the same, and the journey of faith involves staying put. In order to grow mature in Christ, we commit to a life of stability, rooting ourselves in Christ and within a local faith community. Yet, in order to grow mature in Christ, we also commit to ongoing conversion—to journey with Christ and with the local community of faith.

Stability and fidelity involve not only remaining in Christ as we journey together, but also journeying with Christ into ever increasing stability within the community. As Esther de Waal describes the second vow of lifelong conversion,

> It is because I am at home in myself that I can also journey. Having presented us with the promise to stay still and be rooted, Benedict now turns to the second promise, *conversatio morum*, which carries the implication of journeying, moving forward, the quest. It is the one that makes the other possible. This is the paradox.

Other paradoxes in the Benedictine spiritual way of life include the creative tensions between community and solitude, words and silence, human labor and divine grace, dying to live, and becoming poor to find true riches. Part of the genius of Benedictine spirituality is learning to live a balanced life of faith within such creative tensions.

In my years as a pastor, I've seen the greatest spiritual growth among those pilgrims who were willing to meet regularly with others, both one-on-one in mentoring relationships and in small groups that focus upon Scripture and upon Jesus Christ. Only when people know they are truly loved and trusted can the vows of stability and fidelity transform a life. Benedict continues to transform the world today through the gift of fidelity to one another, where we are being transformed within loving relationships in Christ.

THE VOW OF OBEDIENCE IN COMMUNITY

The third Benedictine vow also offers us a creative tension, that of discovering freedom through sacrificing freedom in a life of voluntary submission to God. The vow of obedience stands against the third alternative way of life described by Benedict in chapter one of the *Rule*: those who are self-ruled, living according to their feelings and rejecting structure and authority. According to Benedict, "Their law is what they like to do, whatever strikes their fancy. Anything they believe in and choose, they call holy; anything they dislike, they consider forbidden" (RB, 1.8–9). Most of us, regardless of our age, have wrestled with our relationship with authority and truth. Who is in charge? What or who has authority for my life? How can I know the truth? Is there right and wrong? Such basic questions can leave people feeling uncertain about their identity, their purpose in life, and their relationship to others. Into this uncertainty, Benedict offers a world-changing treasure, the gift of sacrificial love by giving of my life through the vow of obedience.

In the opening few sentences of the *Rule*, Benedict presents "the labor of obedience" as a primary way of life for followers of Christ:

> Listen carefully, my son, to the master's instructions, and attend to them with the ear of your heart. This is advice from a father who loves you; welcome it, and faithfully put it into practice. The labor of obedience will bring you back to him from whom you had drifted through the sloth of disobedience. This message of mine is for you, then, if you are ready to give up your own will, once and for all, and armed with the strong and noble weapons of obedience to do battle for the true King, Christ the Lord. (RB, prologue 1–3)

Benedict opens the *Rule* with an invitation to listen to a father's instructions regarding daily life in a family of faith. At the heart of obedience is the gift of actively listening to the instructions of another laying down my will for yours. "It is only when I remind myself that obedience is *ob-audiens*, listening intently to God rather than listening to my own self," writes de Waal, "that what Benedict is telling me— even though it may still seem difficult—is not impossible, for it is a response of love to love."

Those who hear and put into practice the teachings of Christ are those whose lives will be built securely upon a solid foundation (see Matt. 7:24–27). Those who listen to the words of Christ but refuse to put them into practice will live unstable lives as though building their house upon sand. Jesus taught truth in pictures, telling us that rains will come down, streams will rise, and winds will blow against our lives. How we weather the forces that are certain to beat against our lives depends upon how well we have built our lives through listening to the Lord and putting into practice what we've heard from the Word of God. For Benedict, the way to transform the self-ruled life was through "the labor of obedience"—a labor marked first by active listening "with the ears of the heart," listening to the will of God as expressed through Scripture. More than merely listening to words, obedience involves attending to what we have heard and actively seeking to engage in a new way of life in community based upon the instructions we have received. The four movements of obedience from the prologue of the *Rule* include:

- Listen: open our ears to Christ's instructions.
- Attend: pay attention to Christ's teaching with the "ears of our heart."
- Welcome: accept Christ's word as advice from a "father who loves you."
- Practice: act upon Christ's commands in our daily lives.

This fourfold way of obedience charts the path of Scripture as it enters the ear, is attended to by the mind, is welcomed into the heart, and becomes active in the lifestyle of the hearer. As Kardong relates, "Insistence on concrete action is typical of ancient monasticism, which was more a lifestyle than a theory."

Obedience is not a popular word in contemporary culture. According to Benedictine Prioress Laura Swan, "Our postmodern worldview tends to hold 'obedience' in disdain. The postmodern mind may have no use for the concept at all." Along with the rise of postmodernism in the past decades, the American independent spirit of rugged individualism also flies in the face of obedience. Whether presented to a postmodern twenty-year-old, a forty-year-old corporate-climbing executive, or an eighty-year-old pioneer, the biblical way of obedience remains a strange concept to many in today's culture.

People who become actively involved in a local congregation often bring with them a lifestyle and attitude more influenced by secular culture than by Christ or Scripture. Included in this secular way of life is a rejection of the way of obedience and the refusal to live within loving accountability. In contrast, pilgrims who live according to the way of obedience participate with a community of faith that seeks to actively listen to the Word of God, attend to what we have heard, welcome the instruction, and put Scripture into practice in our daily life together. Again, Laura Swan offers valuable insight:

> The early monastic approach to obedience is rich and complex. Obedience was about listening together, discerning the movement of the Holy Spirit in the life of the individual seeker and in the community. Obedience was to act upon the word received, committing ourselves to one another and to the communal monastic project.

The act of "listening together," as Swan expresses it, is not such a foreign practice in our contemporary culture as it may seem at first. This act can be found in a variety of arenas today, including public schools, military service, team sports, corporate America, and the family. In each of these five arenas, groups of people unite together for a common purpose through the fourfold act of obedience: listening to instructions, attending and receiving these instructions, and putting into practice what they have heard. Without this core practice of communal obedience, each of these settings would face chaos, conflict, and disorganization. Imagine schools where students paid no attention to their teacher. Or consider what troubles would arise on a military base where soldiers ignored the orders of the commanding officer and did their own thing any given day. A team without the authority of a coach who provides clear instructions about how to improve both team and individual performances will seldom see a winning season. The world of corporate business depends upon employees fulfilling the orders and the expectations of executives. Families without discipline and obedience suffer from insecurity and instability.

In the *Rule*, Benedict offers a variety of metaphors to describe the community of faith. Among the many images in the prologue alone, he calls the monastery "a school for the Lord's service" (see RB, prologue 45), a military regiment where faith soldiers "do battle for the true King" (see RB, prologue 3), a team of athletes who "run on the path of God's commandments" (see RB, prologue 49), a workplace with workmen (see RB, prologue 14), and a family where sons and daughters listen to the wise instructions of a parent (see RB, prologue 1).

Five hundred years before Benedict, Paul wrote letters of spiritual formation to Timothy, as a father writing to a son, and employed the same cluster of metaphors of faith: the military, athletics, the workplace, and the family (see 2 Tim. 2:1–6). In all of these metaphors, obedience is understood as a core communal practice.

Benedict was no idealistic dreamer; he was a community realist. He understood the difficulties and the cost of living a life of obedience in community. Regarding the challenges of living such a life of obedience within the monastery, Benedict wrote, "We must, then, prepare our hearts and bodies for the battle of holy obedience to his instructions. What is not possible to us by nature, let us ask the Lord to supply by the help of his grace" (RB, prologue 40–41). The obedience Benedict spoke of within the cloister was the submission of a monk to a mentor. Some people today balk at the thought of submitting their lives to any other human because of the potential abuse of this authority. Without the grace of the Lord working within the life of a community, obedience can certainly be abused or neglected. Neither the abuse of obedience nor its neglect should cause a faith community to avoid the hard work of this basic spiritual commitment. Just because some leaders abuse authority does not mean that all authority should be avoided. People are wise to avoid leaders who themselves refuse to live in loving accountability. As Benedict wrote concerning the accountability of the abbot:

> The abbot must never teach or decree or command anything that would deviate from the Lord's instructions. . . . Let the abbot always remember that at the fearful judgment of God, not only his teaching but also his disciples' obedience will come under scrutiny. . . . Whatever the number of brothers he has in his care, let him realize that on judgment day he will surely have to submit a reckoning to the Lord for all their souls—and indeed for his own as well. (RB, 2.4, 6, 38)

Spiritual leaders are accountable to the Lord, the true head of the church, as well as being accountable to the people over whom they seek to lead. Within the life of a local congregation, pastors and other leaders can live out this commitment to mutual accountability through regular meetings for prayer, spiritual formation, and evaluation. In the Presbyterian polity of church leadership, a local congregation is governed by a group of elders known as the Session. Elders and deacons in a Presbyterian church are elected by the congregation and serve for three-year terms of service. According to the Book of Order, the *rule of life* for the Presbyterian Church, U.S.A., elders and deacons have unique duties:

> It is the duty of elders, individually and jointly, to strengthen and nurture the faith and life of the congregation committed to their charge. Together with the pastor, they should encourage the people in the worship and service of God, equip and renew them for their tasks within the church and for their mission in the world. . . . The office of deacon as set forth in Scripture is one of sympathy, witness, and service after the example of Jesus Christ. It is the duty of deacons, first of all, to minister to those who are in need, to the sick, to the friendless, and to any who may be in distress both within and beyond the community of faith.

These two groups of lay leaders meet monthly for prayer, spiritual formation, and overseeing the various ministries of the church. The moderator of the elders, the pastor, leads the elder team but does not vote. In this balance of spiritual authority, Christ's presence becomes evident through mutual accountability, as the various leaders seek the Lord's guidance and goodwill for the building up of the whole congregation. As Benedict writes in the *Rule*, "Obedience is a blessing to be shown to all, not only to the abbot but also to one another as brothers, since we know that it is by this way of obedience that we go to God" (RB, 71.1–2).

A life of obedience calls us to live under God's guidance as it is revealed among a community of local followers of Christ. In the Benedictine cloister, this life involves obedience to the *Rule*, to the abbot, to the community, and ultimately to Jesus Christ. Jesus boldly declared, "For I have come down from heaven not to do my own will but to do the will of him who sent me" (Jn. 6:38). Christian formation involves attentive listening to Jesus Christ, and doing his will by putting into practice what we have heard.

Through these three lifelong commitments—the vows of stability, fidelity, and obedience—Benedict continues to transform spirituality by deeply influencing the lives of individuals and communities all over the world. Through the vow of stability, Benedict offers the world the gift of well-rooted Christian community from which eternal fruit continues to grow. Through the vow of fidelity, Benedict offers the world the gift of love in community, the love of Christ that alone is able to transform hurting, broken lives. Through the vow of obedience, Benedict continues to transform the world through those who willingly lay down their lives for the sake of others—putting love into action.

One practical way these three vows can deepen the life of a local congregation is to offer them to new members, as they come to join the church, as lifelong commitments made before the people. For those who have decision-making responsibility of welcoming new members in the local church, consider asking people to make a three-fold commitment as they stand before the congregation:

1. COMMITMENT TO STABILITY IN GOD THROUGH CHRIST. Do you commit your life to stability in God through a growing relationship with Jesus Christ as your Lord and Savior, and do you seek to grow together with us in your worship of God, your study of God's Word, and your life of prayer in God?

2. COMMITMENT TO FIDELITY TO CHRIST AND THE CHURCH. Do you commit your life to fidelity to Christ through a growing relationship with the church, welcoming

others as Christ, and seeking in your daily life practical ways
to build up the people of God in love?

3. COMMITMENT OF OBEDIENCE TO CHRIST'S WORK
IN THE WORLD. Do you commit your life in obedience to
Christ to a growing involvement with Christ's work in the
world, and will you try to put into practice the command
of Christ, giving of your time, talents, finances, and indeed
offering your whole life to love others as Christ loves us?

When the vows of stability, fidelity, and obedience become a way
of life among a faith community, the whole body of Christ grows and
builds itself up in faith, hope, and love. We reveal our love for Christ
by putting into practice his commands in our life together. "If you love
me, what I command you will obey" (Jn. 14:15). The return for our
lifelong labor of stability, fidelity, and obedience is God's promised
presence, fruitfulness, and peace. God guides us into this new way of
living year after year. God's Spirit produces the fruit of the Spirit in
our lives, offering refreshment to a hungry and thirsty world. Christ's
gift of peace arises within the hearts of all who live according to God's
Word. As Paul reminds us, "Whatever you have learned or received
or heard from me, or seen in me—put it into practice. And the God of
peace will be with you" (Phil. 4:9).

THE WAY OF BENEDICTINE OBLATION

Monastic candidates still follow in Benedict's footsteps into the
monastic life—by making and keeping lifelong promises of stability, fidelity to monastic life, and obedience. Ask a Benedictine monk
about the preparation necessary for entering into such a life, and he
may reply with this monastic proverb: "The road to the monastery is

seven years long." In today's world, Benedictine monks can prepare for as much as seven years before making their final monastic vow. Over the period of these years of formation, a person begins to learn three vital life lessons: to live together daily with God and others (stability), to be willing to be changed by God and others (fidelity), and to actively listen to God and others (obedience). According to Esther de Waal, Benedictine vows help us

> face a number of very basic demands: the need not to run away, the need to be open to change, the need to listen. They are based on a commitment which is both total and continuing. And yet the paradox is that they bring freedom, true freedom.

Though monasteries have welcomed pilgrims throughout the past fifteen centuries, in the past century there has been a growing movement of people journeying to abbeys for times of renewal. Monasteries welcome thousands upon thousands of seekers every year through their guesthouse doors. Guests are offered a private room, three meals a day, and multiple opportunities for daily communal worship with the monks. More than mere physical repose, the cloister welcomes thirsty travelers to drink from the deep well of contemplative Christian spirituality. Active people discover through the silence and solitude of the monastery such refreshment that they yearn for more of this new way of life upon returning home. As the Lord welcomed ancient Israel long ago, "With joy you will draw water from wells of salvation" (Isa. 12:3), so monasteries all over the world welcome pilgrims to come into the quiet of the cloister and drink from a deep well. In chapter eleven, I offer a "User's Guide to Going on a Monastic Retreat," an essay offering personal and practical guidance for enjoying such a time away at a monastery.

One of the other growing movements among Benedictine monasticism is called oblation. An Oblate is someone who promises to live according to Benedictine principles as much as possible according to their station in life outside the walls of the monastery. Today, there are an estimated twenty-five thousand Benedictine Oblates worldwide, with more joining every year. The mission statement for Oblates of Mount Angel Abbey, a Benedictine monastery in Mount Angel, Oregon, describes the purpose:

> Formed by the Benedictine monastic tradition, oblates of Mount Angel Abbey seek God in Christian discipleship in the world. By obedience to Catholic teaching, faithfulness to liturgical prayer and continual conversion of life according to the Holy Rule of Saint Benedict, oblates seek union with God and growth in charity toward one's neighbor. This work is undertaken in spiritual communion with the monks of Mount Angel Abbey with the desire that in all things God may be glorified, and that together we may come to life everlasting. Amen.

Like preparation for monastic profession, an Oblate takes a full year of preparation before making the lifelong promise of oblation. This promise is made before God and the whole monastic community during morning worship. As Oblates, people seek to live their lives according to Benedictine principles as expressed in the five paths in this book. Each Oblate is associated with a specific community, both through daily prayers and annual renewal retreats. The root of the word *oblation* means to make an offering. Oblates offer themselves to the Lord and to service for the Lord in the world—as living sacrifices they seek to follow in the footsteps of Jesus.

In Benedict's time, people brought their children to the monastery as a living offering of their lives. Thus, in the *Rule*, readers discover instructions regarding the care, discipline, and instruction of children living within the cloister. As the Benedictine movement spread across Europe, artists, growers, and merchants became actively involved in the life of the local abbey, providing food, goods, and supplies. In return, the monks sought to instruct these laypeople in the ways of Christ. Though the Benedictine order never formally recognized a third order for nonmonastics, as found among the Franciscans, the Benedictine Oblates have served in this capacity for centuries, bringing the wisdom and daily practices of Benedictine spirituality into homes, marketplaces, and cities.

Oblate spirituality grows out of the same threefold promise of stability, fidelity, and obedience. While this threefold promise is worked out in various ways to adapt to varieties of settings in which Oblates live, the core remains the same: a commitment to be rooted in Christ and in Christian community (stability), a commitment to lifelong conversion in Christ within a faith community (fidelity), and the willingness to listen, learn, and live according to Christ's principles in the world (obedience). Through their daily prayer and work, Oblates seek to reveal the peace of Christ in their manner of living as they walk the paths of Benedictine spirituality. As Benedict declares in the *Rule*, "See how the Lord in his love shows us the way of life. Clothed then with faith and the performance of good works, let us set out on this way, with the Gospel for our guide" (RB, prologue 20–21).

TAKING STEPS
INTO CHRISTIAN FORMATION

from Chapter Eight

- Consider areas of instability in your local community. Write out a list of these and share them with a friend. Consider ways of bringing stability to people whose lives are uncertain or unstable at this time.

- If you have never joined a local church, consider doing so this year. Make your public declaration of commitment to Christ and become involved in the life and ministry of this church family.

- Consider John Donne's view of humanity: "No man is an island, entire of itself; every other man is a piece of the continent, a part of the main." List three ways this perspective could change your relationships with others.

- Enter into an intentional relationship with a Christian from another nation. Do this through e-mail, through a computer social network, or through regular mail. Contact a person from another nation and begin exchanging letters, ideas, and faith encouragement.

- Meet regularly in a spiritual mentor relationship with another believer.

- Meet regularly with a small group that focuses upon spiritual growth through Scripture and through Jesus Christ.

- Listen to Christ's instructions. Attend to Christ's teachings. Welcome Christ's words. Practice Christ's way of life.

- If you are involved with leadership within a local church, consider changing the way you bring people into active membership, taking time for Christian formation in their lives, and asking them to make lifelong commitments of stability, fidelity, and obedience as part of their active membership.

CHAPTER 9

Five Case Studies of Christian Formation

Maps, books, and trail guides offer valuable assistance in planning a journey, but there comes a time to fold up the maps, set down the books, and start hiking on the path. Throughout the past fifteen centuries, many communities of faith have followed in Benedict's footsteps, seeking to live a life of faith together, under a common *rule of life*. In this chapter we look at five case studies, assessing five faith communities from the past century that have walked together in intentional Christian formation by adopting a *rule of life* for their shared life in Christ. When I speak of a *rule of life*, I'm referring to a short, written document that guides the life of a Christian community. Longer than a church mission statement, this *rule of life* offers biblical principles and practical guidelines for our common life in Christ as lived in the community of faith. Each of the five case studies in this chapter reveal faithfulness to a *rule of life*. Each of the five Christian communities have sought to live out Benedict's vision of intentional Christian life together. In the following chapter, we'll explore ways of writing such a *rule of life* within the setting of a local church. My hope in presenting these five brief case studies is that you glean practical ideas for developing a community *rule of life* with other fellow pilgrims in your local faith community. The five case studies include the Finkenwald Seminary of Germany in the 1930s, the Iona Community of Scotland, the Taizé Community of France, the Northumbria Community of England, and the New Monasticism movement of North America.

FINKENWALD SEMINARY OF GERMANY

Perhaps the most important book on the church written in the twentieth century is Dietrich Bonhoeffer's *Life Together*, published in 1938 and written as a *rule of life* to help guide the underground seminary community of Finkenwald. While serving as pastor of two German-speaking congregations in London, Dietrich Bonhoeffer received an invitation to oversee a clandestine seminary to train pastors for the Confessing Church of Germany. For the next two years, Bonhoeffer and several dozen seminarians lived at Finkenwald, in the north of Germany, exploring communal living according to a common *rule of life* under the guidance of Scripture. The community was disbanded in 1937 when it was discovered and shut down by the Gestapo. By November 1937, twenty-seven students from this illegal seminary had been arrested by the German state police. During the few years the seminary was in operation, Bonhoeffer documented the theology and practice of the Finkenwald community in *Gemeinsames Leben*, or *Life Together*, a guidebook for what he called a "new type of monasticism."

Christian life together, according to Bonhoeffer, "means community through Jesus Christ and in Jesus Christ. No Christian community is more or less than this." As a Lutheran theologian and pastor, Bonhoeffer centered the Finkenwald community on the grace of God in Jesus Christ and the finished work of Christ on the cross. "One is a brother to another only through Jesus Christ. I am a brother to another person through what Jesus Christ did for me and to me; the other person has become a brother to me through what Jesus Christ did for him."

After Bonhoeffer laid out the foundational theology for Christian community, he built upon that foundation by describing the practice of daily life together in Christian formation. The day begins by practicing such community disciplines as morning devotions, praying the Psalms, reading the Scriptures together, singing and praying together, and table fellowship. Bonhoeffer proceeds into "the day's work" by describing the positive impact of Morning Prayer upon the rest of the day. The day with others also involves fellowship at noonday and at the evening table, and concludes with last devotions at night. "The prayer of the Psalms, a hymn, and common prayer close the day, as they opened it."

In addition to "the day with others," Bonhoeffer also describes "the day alone," in which community members practice such disciplines as solitude and silence, meditation, prayer, and intercession. Like Benedict, Bonhoeffer expressed great concern for "holding one's tongue." Both leaders recognized the great danger in Christian community of grumbling, gossip, and judging others with our words. Also like Benedict, Bonhoeffer seasoned his guidebook with an abundance of Scripture verses to support his case for Christian community life. For example, in writing on holding one's tongue, Bonhoeffer quotes from Psalm 50:20–21, James 4:11–12, and Ephesians 4:29. In addition to the spiritual discipline of the restraint of speech, Bonhoeffer exhorts his community to practice the ministries of meekness, listening to one another, helpfulness, bearing one another's burdens, proclaiming the Word person to person, as well as the acceptance of authority.

In the final section of *Life Together*, Bonhoeffer articulated the twin practices of confession and Communion as central to all Christian community. Both of these practices are rooted in the work of Christ who forgave our sins, called us to confess our sins to one another, and gave us the sacrament of Communion to strengthen our faith in our common life together. Bonhoeffer wrote of "breaking through" into this new way of community living: "Sin demands to have a man by himself. It withdraws him from the community. . . . Since the confession of sin is made in the presence of a Christian brother, the last stronghold of self-justification is abandoned."

As we confess our sins to one another, we emerge into a new life of certainty and joy through the power of the Cross.

The joy shared in community is best expressed through what Bonhoeffer calls "the joyful Sacrament," the Lord's Supper. "Here the community has reached its goal. Here joy in Christ and his community is complete. The life of Christians together under the Word has reached its perfection in the sacrament." Bonhoeffer's *Life Together* presents a guidebook for Christian life together, a twentieth-century *rule of life* for the practice of intentional Christian formation in community.

Though the Finkenwald Seminary only endured two years before the Gestapo discovered this clandestine community, the lessons discovered and practiced there have strengthened the church through the clarity and Christ-centered vision of Christian community as expressed through Bonhoeffer's writings. In a letter to his brother in 1935, at the beginning of his Finkenwald experiment, Bonhoeffer described his vision of this ancient, yet new way of life in Christ.

> The restoration of the church will surely come only from a new type of monasticism which has nothing in common with the old but a complete lack of compromise in a life lived in accordance with the Sermon on the Mount in the discipleship of Christ. I think it is time to gather people together to do this.

LESSONS FROM *LIFE TOGETHER* AND THE FINKENWALD COMMUNITY

- Christian community is only through Jesus Christ and in Jesus Christ.
- Our life together as a Christian community involves specific spiritual practices, including morning devotions, praying the Psalms, reading the Scriptures together, singing and praying together, and table fellowship at noonday and in the evening.
- Our life in Christ also calls us away from community for individual spiritual practices, including solitude, silence, meditation, prayer, and intercession.
- Grave dangers to any Christian community involve such troubles as grumbling, gossip, and judging others with our words. It is better to hold our tongue than engage in such things.
- The two habits central to all Christian community are mutual confession and celebration of Communion, the joyful sacrament of the Lord's Supper.
- True Christian community involves a "new type of monasticism," that of a "life lived in accordance to the Sermon on the Mount."

IONA COMMUNITY OF SCOTLAND

In 1938, the same year Bonhoeffer published *Life Together*, George MacLeod, a forty-three-year-old minister of the Church of Scotland, abandoned his parish ministry in the Clydeside dock district of Glasgow, Scotland, and went to the Isle of Iona. MacLeod took six unemployed ship workers and six young clergymen from the Church of Scotland with him. Together, with these first twelve men, he founded the Iona Community. This community of men rebuilt part of the ruined thirteenth-century Benedictine Iona Abbey as they experimented with communal Christian living under a common *rule of life*.

Iona has been the cradle of Scottish Christianity since 563, the year that Columba (521–97) settled the island, after being exiled from Ireland. With a band of twelve disciples, Columba sailed across the Irish Sea to land on the Isle of Iona, off the western shores of Scotland. Columba founded a monastery on Iona in the late sixth century and it was from this missionary base that he traveled widely across Scotland and won the highland chieftains and their people to Jesus Christ.

Though the current population of the Isle of Iona is just over one hundred residents, tens of thousands of pilgrims visit the sacred site every year in order to trace the footsteps of Columba and those who followed after him. These pilgrims come to visit the medieval abbey, the graveyard, and the natural setting of the island itself. They are also welcomed by the MacLeod Center and visit the retreat center, gift shop, and bookstore run by the Iona Community. The Iona Community is an ecumenical and international community of Christians who are seeking to live according to the vision of Columba and George MacLeod through intentional Christian community life together, seeking the peace of Christ and justice in society.

The members of the Iona Community share a common *rule of life*, focusing upon classic spiritual disciplines such as daily prayer and reading the Bible, mutual sharing of life together in community, accountability in the use of money and time, working together with acts of justice and peace in society, and seeking to live in harmony with creation. Over the past seven decades, the Iona Community has been officially connected to the Church of Scotland, and features several centers in Glasgow and on the islands of Iona and Mull. The membership is international and represents many Christian denominations around the world. One of the creative aspects of the Iona Community is the variety of levels of commitments encouraged among the participants. These include members, associate members, staff members, friends of Iona, volunteers, and intercessors in the Iona prayer circle. All of these people actively seek to carry out MacLeod's vision of living out the life-transforming gospel of Jesus Christ in community in today's world.

LESSONS FROM THE IONA COMMUNITY

- There is wisdom in bringing together manual laborers and ministers for the building of Christian community. Both have important lessons to learn from one another.
- Christian community is intended to become a base for reaching out into the wider world and for birthing other Christian communities.
- A *rule of life* may include such community habits as daily prayer, reading the Bible together, mutual sharing, accountability for use of time and money, and meeting together regularly to share life.
- Christian community requires both reflection and action in Christ's ways of justice, peace, and caring for creation.
- Christian community offers a variety of levels of participation and commitment for people seeking to become involved in the community: members, associate members, friends, volunteers, intercessors, and staff.
- It is helpful to visit a community. Consider making a sacred pilgrimage to Iona to soak in the beauty and simplicity of

REM*fresh*

RECEIVE $10 toward your next purchase of REMfresh® on REMFRESH.COM

Doctors are noting how their patients are benefiting from REMfresh®.

You can help sleep research by adding your feedback to this growing body of experience with REMfresh®. In this way, our research will be able to accumulate the collective experience of users of REMfresh® and share it in the appropriate venue.

Please visit **REMfreshOffer.com** and complete our short, 60 second survey about your experience and you will receive a $10.00 coupon good toward your next purchase of REMfresh®.

Make your contribution to Sleep Research.

Thank you,
The Physician's Seal Team
Innovators of REMfresh®

REMfreshOffer.com

REM*fresh*

...cribed by MacLeod as "a thin ...se to earth. For more informa- ...munity, see www.iona.org.uk.

...E

...d began the Iona community, ...wiss Reformed Christian, rode ...Switzerland to the small village ...mother had grown up. There ...prayer, and welcome Jewish ...Easter Day in 1949, the first ...unity professed lifelong vows ...of what has since become an ...community. Since its humble ...has grown and expanded to ...rthodox, Roman Catholics, and ...y-five nationalities. Community members make a commitment to a life of celibacy, poverty, and fidelity to the community.

During the winter of 1952, Brother Roger went on an extended silent retreat to write a common *rule of life* for the Taizé Community, publishing the *Rule of Taizé* in 1953. This is a "living" document that guides the daily life of the community to this day. Brother Roger wrote in the preamble to the *Rule of Taizé*, "This Rule contains only the minimum necessary for a community seeking to build itself in Christ, and to give itself up to a common service of God." The *Rule of Taizé*, a brief document of less than four thousand words, includes four sections, three of which are "The Acts of Community," "The Spiritual Disciplines," and "The Vows." The communal acts of the

Taizé Community include prayer, the common meal, and the council. At council the Taizé Community meets to discuss issues facing the whole community. "The purpose of the council is to seek all the light possible concerning the will of Christ for the march forward of the community." Spiritual disciplines include meditation, silence, joy, simplicity, and mercy. Taizé brothers make lifelong vows of celibacy, poverty, and acceptance of authority. The fourth section of the *Rule of Taizé* includes chapters on mission travel, welcoming new members, and welcoming guests. As a practical way of living out the *Rule of Taizé* in their commitment to caring for guests, the Taizé Community welcomes several thousand guests every week in the summer and hundreds of guests during the rest of the year. These guests are invited to enter into the daily rhythm of communal worship, work, prayer, and study.

In 1986, Pope John Paul II visited the Taizé Community and spoke to the thousands of young people gathered for that audience. He encouraged his young audience as he expressed the unique gift of the Taizé Community:

> Like you, pilgrims and friends of the community, the pope is only passing through. But one passes through Taizé as one passes close to a spring of water. The traveler stops, quenches his thirst, and continues on his way. The brothers of the community, you know, do not want to keep you. They want, in prayer and silence, to enable you to drink the living water promised by Christ, to know his joy, to discern his presence, to respond to his call, then to set out again to witness to his love and to serve your brothers and sisters in your parishes, your schools, your universities, and in all your places of work.

LESSONS FROM THE TAIZÉ COMMUNITY

- Writing a brief *rule of life* will help guide your life with others.
- A church *rule of life* may include equivalent sections from the *Rule of Taizé*:
  - The acts of the community including prayer, meals and council
  - Spiritual disciplines including meditation, silence, joy, simplicity, and mercy
  - Community vows including stability, fidelity, and obedience
  - Hospitality including mission, welcoming new members, and welcoming guests.
- Christian community can unite people of different Christian backgrounds into one family that includes Protestants, Catholics, and Orthodox believers, as well as people from a wide variety of nationalities and language groups.
- Starting a Taizé-like worship service in your community, using Taizé worship resources easily ordered through www.giamusic.com, can be a vehicle for drawing new people to your church. In January 2006, Community Presbyterian Church began such a Taizé worship service twice a month on Sunday evenings. After three years, we have seen many new people coming to the church as well as a renewed interest in such disciplines as meditation, silence, and singing the Psalms.
- For those who are able to do so, consider making a sacred pilgrimage to the Taizé community in France to spend a week sharing life together with this community and with the thousands of other prayer retreatants who come every week. For more information on the Taizé Community, see www.taize.fr/en.

NORTHUMBRIA COMMUNITY OF ENGLAND

Though the Northumbria Community was founded less than two decades ago, its roots lie deep in the soil of the Holy Island of Lindisfarne in northern England. In 635, an Irish monk named Aidan was sent from Iona Abbey in Scotland to minister to the people of Northumbria. By invitation of King Oswald, Aidan founded the first monastery in the region on the Island of Lindisfarne. Twice a day, this tidal island is cut off from mainland by high tide. Today, when driving over at low tide, many signs warn guests to keep an eye on tide charts so as not to be cut off. The genius of Aidan's choice for his community is connected to the rhythm of the tides that allow set times every day for time alone with God as well as set time daily for time together with pilgrims and guests.

For sixteen years, Aidan ministered as an evangelist for the gospel of Jesus Christ to the people of Northumbria. He died there in 651. Aidan was a humble and gentle missionary and was widely loved and respected by the people of Northumbria. King Oswald gave him a white stallion for his mission, but Aidan gladly gave it to the first beggar family he met. When Oswald confronted him about this act, Aidan rebuked the king for loving the son of a mare more than the son of Mary. Aidan walked from village to village, always traveling by foot. Willing to visit with people face to face along the road, he often entered poor peasant homes to offer spiritual and physical aid while gently accepting people in the love of Jesus Christ.

In April 2008, Dr. Ian Bradley, professor in practical theology and church history at the University of St. Andrews, made a proposal to the English parliament to consider making Aidan the new patron saint of the United Kingdom. Bradley's proposal stands on sound historic foundations. Along with St. Augustine of Canterbury, St. Aidan is widely considered the apostle to the English. Unlike St. George or St. Andrew, the patron saints of England and Scotland respectively, who never set foot in what is now Great Britain, Aidan was born in Ireland, lived in Scotland, and spent the final sixteen years of his life in northern England. After Aidan's death, Lindisfarne Abbey became one of the most influential missionary bases in all of England, spreading Christianity among the English-speaking people during the medieval period. Commenting on Aidan's lasting influence, Bradley notes, "The monastery which he established at Lindisfarne was to prove almost as important a missionary centre as its mother house at Iona. From it monks penetrated far down into the areas of England held by the pagan Angles and Saxons."

The Northumbria Community of England, following in Aidan's footsteps, seeks to live out a new form of monasticism according to the Sermon on the Mount "united in heart by our common commitment to our vows, in which we say 'YES' to Availability and Vulnerability, and in being companions together in Community." The foundations for the Northumbria Community date back to 1976, the year that Andy Raine went to live on the Holy Island of Lindisfarne, where he began to practice a daily rhythm of Celtic liturgical prayer. In 1990, John and Linda Skinner joined with Roy Searle to formally establish the Northumbria Community according to a community *rule of life*, and they based this community at Hetton Hall, on the mainland near Lindisfarne. Included in the community rule of Northumbria is a twofold commitment: to availability and vulnerability. Community members promise to be available to God through daily time alone and together in contemplative prayer. They also seek to be available to one another and to others through a ministry of hospitality, intercessory prayer, and mission. The commitment of availability calls community members to be teachable and to unite through communal disciplines of prayer, prayerful Scripture study, mutual accountability, and soul friendships. Dispersed across the landscape of northern England and Scotland, the Northumbria Community commits to gathering together monthly for common meals, study, and worship using *Celtic Daily Prayer*. Community members meet together in many house communities around the world and through online connections as they seek to live "openly among people as 'Church without walls.'"

LESSONS FROM LINDISFARNE AND THE NORTHUMBRIA COMMUNITY

- A community rhythm offers set times each week for time alone with God, as well as time together with others.
- A true faith community becomes a mission-sending base, from which to send out many people like Aidan who bring the Good News of Jesus Christ through their humble and gentle spirit.
- A helpful community *rule of life* includes basic values such as being available (to God and to one another) and being vulnerable to one another in humility.
- Commitment to such ministries as hospitality, intercessory prayer, and mission is part of a healthy community.
- Commit to such disciplines as communal prayer, prayerful Scripture study, mutual accountability, and soul friendships.
- Utilizing a prayer book such as *Celtic Daily Prayer* unites the community of faith in regular weekly times of worship and prayer, both within a church building and also in homes.

- It is important to seek creative ways to live openly as followers of Jesus—as a "church without walls." For more information on the Northumbria Community, see www .northumbriacommunity.org.

THE NEW MONASTICISM MOVEMENT OF NORTH AMERICA

During a gathering in Durham, North Carolina, in 2004, a group of over sixty Christians met to discuss the defining marks of the "new monasticism" movement. The title "new monasticism" is attributed to Dietrich Bonhoeffer and his Finkenwald experiment in the 1930s. In the United States, this movement involves an informal network of "some 100 groups that describe themselves as both evangelical and monastic." The New Monasticism Gathering in 2004 agreed upon the following twelve marks to define the new monasticism movement:

1. Relocation to the abandoned places of Empire.
2. Sharing economic resources with fellow community members and the needy among us.
3. Hospitality to the stranger.
4. Lament for racial divisions within the church and our communities combined with the active pursuit of a just reconciliation.
5. Humble submission to Christ's body, the church.
6. Intentional formation in the way of Christ and the rule of the community along the lines of the old novitiate.
7. Nurturing common life among members of intentional community.
8. Support for celibate singles alongside monogamous married couples and their children.

9. Geographical proximity to community members who share a common rule of life.

10. Care for the plot of God's earth given to us along with support of our local economies.

11. Peacemaking in the midst of violence and conflict resolution within communities.

12. Commitment to a disciplined contemplative life.

Those who gathered in 2004 summarized their time together with the following benediction for the practice of Christian formation. "May God give us grace by the power of the Holy Spirit to discern rules for living that will help us embody these marks in our local contexts as signs of Christ's kingdom for the sake of God's world."

The New Monasticism Gathering represented Christian communities throughout the United States: Catholics, Pentecostals, Evangelicals, and many mainline Protestant denominations. Though these communities vary widely in style and structure, they share a common commitment to communal life together in Christ and a daily commitment to follow Christ together through practicing disciplines in community. Like the Benedictine order, "new monastic" communities across the United States have largely been founded and governed by lay Christians, and like Benedictine monasteries, they focus upon personal and communal daily prayer. In addition, these "new monastic" communities practice Benedictine-style hospitality, as they welcome people as they would Christ with little regard to economic, racial, or social factors. Most of these communities work prayerfully for peace and justice through Jesus Christ, especially for the poor in their immediate communities. Like Benedict's cloistered monks, these various communities seek to live out the claims of the gospel of Jesus Christ and the example of the early church in the book of Acts. Frequently found among these "new monastic" communities is a communal approach to finances, possessions, and meals.

Among the new monastic communities in the United States, there also exist distinctive traits that set them apart from traditional Benedictine monasticism. These include: married and celibates dwelling communally in the same home; a wide variety of organizational structures without one single *rule of life* to govern the whole movement; much greater latitude for individual freedom apart from authority than would typically be found in a Benedictine monastery; an openness to ecumenical membership that includes Roman Catholics, Protestants, and even non-Christians; and a global perspective for missions and service.

One can easily overlook, when looking at just one of these houses, the rise of community approaches to spiritual formation across the continent over the past two decades. Alasdair McIntyre wrote in his 1984 book *After Virtue*, "We are waiting not for a Godot, but for another—and doubtless very different—St. Benedict." Writing as a professor of moral and political philosophy, McIntyre, like Bonhoeffer fifty years earlier, envisioned a new movement where communal moral practices unite people through a new kind of Benedictine support system. Perhaps the growing numbers of Christian communities that make up the "new monasticism" movement are just what McIntyre envisioned—another St. Benedict coming in the guise of intentional Christian community life together.

In an essay titled "Remonking the Church," featured in the September 2005 issue of *Christianity Today*, the editors asked if a Protestant form of monasticism would help free evangelicalism from its cultural captivity. First printed in 1988, this editorial mentions three leading evangelical voices in the West, all of which speak of the same "new monastic" movement as the hope for church renewal in the late twentieth century. John R. Stott, one of the leading statesmen of British evangelicalism; Richard Halverson, former Senate Chaplain; and Fuller Theological Seminary president Richard Mouw all mention an interest in an evangelical Protestant form of monasticism, or what Mouw calls a "remonasticization" of the church.

Several possible "remonking" lifestyles offered by the editors of *Christianity Today* include young celibate singles living in the same home in order to better facilitate intentional Christian formation; families moving into the same neighborhood in order to meet daily for common worship and spiritual formation; or retirees choosing to move to live among other retirees who share the same commitment to community approaches to formation and compassionate service in the world.

LESSONS FROM THE NEW MONASTICISM MOVEMENT OF NORTH AMERICA

- Some of the twelve marks of "new monasticism" listed on pages 165–66 may challenge your community of faith to grow closer to Jesus Christ over the period of one year.
- These twelve marks are a good reference point for writing a *rule of life* within your local congregation. For more information on the new monasticism movement, see their website at www.newmonasticism.org.
- The twelve marks of new monasticism are a good basis for members of a study group, home group, or leadership team to ask each other the following life-application questions:
  - Where are the abandoned places in our community and region?

- How are we currently sharing economic resources with others, especially with the needy in our community?
- When and how are we offering hospitality to strangers?
- How have we helped to heal racial divisions within the church and in our world?
- What steps are we taking together to live a life of humble submission to the body of Christ?
- How are we intentionally growing together in Christ through Christian formation?
- In what ways are we nurturing our common life together?
- When and how do we support celibate singles alongside monogamous married couples and families?
- Have we committed to living near each other, and what changes has this brought in our community life together?
- Are we caring for God's earth and supporting the local economies in our area?
- Are we involved in Christ's work of peacemaking in our community and world?
- Have we committed ourselves to a disciplined contemplative life?
- What does this life look like in our community?

How might the five communities mentioned above help you and your local congregation grow closer to Jesus Christ in your life together here in the twenty-first century? What lessons have you learned from these five case studies? Which of these communities do you want to learn more about this year? It is one thing to learn how people lived for Jesus Christ in the past. It is quite another matter putting this into practice among fellow pilgrims to establish a Christlike way of life. How might we practice anew in our time the timeless principles and practical ways of Christian formation discovered in *The Rule of St. Benedict*? What guidance might Benedictine spirituality offer to a local church for deepening life together in Christ? We now turn to the possible answers to these questions.

TAKING STEPS
INTO CHRISTIAN FORMATION

from Chapter Nine

- Choose one lesson from Dietrich Bonhoeffer's *Life Together* or from the Finkenwald community to put into practice in your life.

- Choose one lesson from Columba's life, George MacLeod's life, or the Iona Community and put it into practice in your life.

- Choose one lesson from Brother Roger's life or the Taizé Community to put into practice in your life.

- Choose one lesson from Aidan's life, the Holy Isle of Lindisfarne, or the Northumbria Community to put into practice in your life.

- Choose one lesson from the "twelve marks of new monasticism" or from the new monasticism movement to put into practice in your life.

CHAPTER 10

A Guide for Christian Formation in a Local Chuch

Benedict concludes the *Rule* with an explanation of why he wrote his guidebook. "The reason we have written this rule is that, by observing it in monasteries, we can show that we have some degree of virtue and the beginning of monastic life" (RB, 73.1). Trail guidebooks are intended to help people walk the trails described in the guidebook. The opening sentence of the last chapter of the *Rule* paraphrased for the local church might help people in congregations better understand the wisdom found along the paths of Christian spirituality:

> The reason we have written this guidebook for Christian formation is that by practicing the Christian life together in a local congregation, we can show that we have, to some degree, become more Christlike in our manner of living and have truly begun to be spiritually transformed in our life together in Christ. (RB, 73.1, paraphrased by the author)

This transformation occurs gradually as people commit together to this shared way of life. As the psalmist gladly declares, "Blessed are those whose strength is in you, who have set their hearts on pilgrimage" (Ps. 84:5). Like bookends,

Benedict opens and closes the *Rule* with pilgrimage metaphors, binding the *Rule* together as a life guidebook with his vision of life with God as a journey. In the prologue, Benedict paraphrases Jesus' words from John 12:35 with a journey image of faith. *"Run while you have the light of life, that the darkness of death may not overtake you* (Jn. 12:35)" (RB, prologue 13). In the prologue to the *Rule*, he also invites us to "set out on this way," *"walk without blemish* (Ps. 15:2)," "not run away from the road that leads to salvation," "progress in this way of life and in faith," and "run on the path of God's commandments" (see RB, prologue 21, 25, 48–49). He picks up the pilgrimage metaphor once again in the final chapter of the *Rule*, where he writes of being led "to the very heights of perfection," of "hastening toward your heavenly home," and setting out "for the loftier summits" (see RB, 73.2, 8–9). In all these images, Benedict understood faith as a lifelong pilgrimage that requires many steps of faith in our life together in Christ.

While it is clear that members of a local church are not cenobitic monks living in a monastery, it has been asserted throughout this book that Benedict's vision for monasticism has much to offer us today with regard to Christian formation in community. Benedictine spirituality invites us to develop maturity in Christ through practical steps of faith. How might members of a congregation grow deeper in their life together through this ancient way of spirituality? What are the steps we may take to "progress in this way of life and in faith" (RB, prologue 49)?

In the prologue of the *Rule*, Benedict offers several specific steps for Christian formation: "First of all, every time you begin a good work, you must pray to him most earnestly to bring it to perfection. . . . Let us get up then, at long last, for the Scriptures rouse us. . . .

The Lord waits for us daily to translate into action, as we should, his holy teachings" (RB, prologue 4, 8, 35).

1. Pray together.
2. Listen to Scripture together.
3. Serve others together by putting into action what we have heard from the Lord.

How might a ministry of Christian formation be developed within a local church? We begin with prayer, Scripture study, and putting into practice the truths and principles learned from the Word. When we seek to bring about new approaches to spiritual formation within a local church, we walk humbly with God, doing all we can to build up the church through prayerful support of pastors and lay leaders. As a pastor who has served the church for a quarter of a century, I greatly value laypeople within the local church who seek to live out the gospel of Jesus Christ through their daily lives. When such wise and mature people bring to me their heart concerns and visions, I prayerfully seek the counsel of the Holy Spirit and the shared wisdom of the elders of the church. Maybe the Lord is leading us to transform the way we are to live our shared life together as followers of Jesus Christ. Maybe this year is the year for rebuilding and renewing the church according to principles based in the Word of God.

I invite you to consider with me some guidelines for developing a community *rule of life* for a local congregation. These guidelines are written primarily for pastors and lay leaders within the local church, but they offer a theological and historical vision of life together in Christian community, as well as giving practical steps for developing better ways of growing together in Christ. What follows is a sample implementation guide for introducing Christian formation in a local congregation. This guide follows a three-year plan, with active involvement from the clergy, lay leaders, and members. If the organization of this three-year guide does not match the pattern of leadership or decision making in your congregation, feel free to tailor this outline to better meet your needs and practices.

A THREE-YEAR GUIDE TO WRITING A *RULE OF LIFE* FOR A LOCAL CONGREGATION

YEAR ONE. In January of Year One, at a congregation meeting, have the pastor lay out the following three-year plan for Christian formation within the congregation. Each person may be asked to sign a covenant agreement, promising to "progress in this way of life and in faith" (see RB, prologue 49) as we journey together into Christian formation. Beginning in February of Year One, pastors and lay leaders meet together monthly to discuss the paths and practices presented in this book. The goal is to better understand Christian formation, especially as lived out within an intentional community of faith. A group study guide is provided below.

YEAR TWO. In January of Year Two, clergy and lay leaders meet together early in the year. At this meeting, they begin the six-month process of writing a *rule of life* for the congregation. If your local congregation already has a working mission statement, copies of it are made available at this meeting. A mission statement is a brief written statement, often thirty to fifty words in length, expressing God's purpose and mission for the congregation. If you do not have a mission statement, the first step at this January Year Two meeting could be to identify congregational core values—those five to ten central truths, principles, and practices that define your life as a congregation. Write these out on a big board and discuss them together, and provide passages of Scripture that support each core value.

In laying the foundation for writing a *rule of life* for a local church, pastors and lay leaders are wise to emphasize the importance of rooting this document in Scripture, centering this *rule of life* upon Jesus Christ, and tailoring it for people who are new to life in Christ. First, a *rule of life* needs to draw it's principles from Scripture. Throughout *The Rule of St. Benedict*, readers find hundreds of references to Scripture. Benedict wove the written Word of God into nearly every page of his guidebook for Christian formation. Of course, the best guide for spiritual growth in the local church is Scripture.

Secondly, a *rule of life* needs to focus the congregation upon the person of Jesus Christ. As Benedict declared, "Let them prefer nothing whatever to Christ, and may he bring us all together to everlasting life" (RB, 72.1–12). Benedict keeps Christ at the center of his guidebook for Christian formation. Every aspect of our shared life as a local church needs to point us to the head of the church, Jesus Christ.

Third, a congregational *rule of life* needs to be written for beginners in the spiritual life, as Benedict described his writing as "this little rule that we have written for beginners" (RB, 73.8). In writing a *rule of life* for a local church, leaders are wise to temper the writing with God's gentleness, offering people a guidebook of grace, writing with a moderate voice, embracing all levels of Christian maturity, including beginners along the way of Christ. As we heard in the Taizé Community case study, Brother Roger offered the following wisdom concerning writing a *rule of life*:

it needs to contain "only the minimum necessary for a community seeking to build itself in Christ, and to give itself up to a common service of God."

Utilizing your church mission statement or list of core values, orient the group to the nature of a *rule of life* for congregations. Read aloud the prologue from *The Rule of St. Benedict*. Outline the seven basic sections of the *Rule*: community essentials, a life of prayer and worship, guidance and leadership, ordinary life together in the community, sacred study of Scripture, hospitality, and community commitments for Christian formation. Following Benedict's lead, a contemporary guidebook for Christian formation in a local church might include the following sections.

SECTION ONE. The first main section of a *rule of life* includes a prologue, offering a theological vision for Christian formation in community. Consider the opening section of Bonhoeffer's *Life Together* when beginning to write this first main section. This section also lays the biblical foundation for spiritual essentials necessary for life together within the local church. These essentials may include such basics as the theology and practice of spiritual leadership, patterns for community life, tools for spiritual formation that help people live a life of love, the place of obedience, and steps into a life of walking humbly with God and with others.

SECTION TWO. The second section presents the main body of the rule. This section offers guidance along the five paths, or communal practices: communal prayer, spiritual leadership, ordinary spirituality, *lectio divina*, and hospitality.

SECTION THREE. The final section contains approaches to church membership, including the formation process for joining the church, lifelong commitments for active participation in this congregation, and lifelong Christian formation in community.

Early in Year Two, the elders along with the pastor should appoint a small group of wise "scribes" who will work together on behalf of the whole congregation over the next several months and write a rough draft of a *rule of life* that follows this basic Benedictine pattern. Include in this small group a representative of the elders (or other elected lay leadership team), as well as a member of the pastoral staff. Include others from the congregation to gather around these "scribes" and commission them by prayer and blessing.

Over the next several months, this small group of scribes should meet regularly to work its way through each section and draft a simple, scriptural, Christ-centered vision and practice for Christian formation in the local church. This group of scribes may draw upon language used in the *rule of life* from such communities as mentioned above: Bonhoeffer's *Life Together*, the *Rule of Taizé*, the common rules of the Iona Community and the Northumbria Community, as well as the twelve marks of the new monasticism movement. When the *rule of life* has been completed in rough draft form, call the leaders together to listen to a reading of the rough draft. This might happen in the summer of Year Two. Have the group offer constructive comments and suggestions for improvements. Invite questions and comments. Search the Scriptures. Review your mission statement. Ask people to say aloud what they like most about the writing, and also what they think may improve the writing. Ask someone to keep notes from this meeting. The spirit of this meeting should be positive, constructive, and gracious. At the end of the discussion, offer prayers together for the rewriting of the *rule of life*. Send the scribal team off with the blessing of the leaders of the church to complete the writing process.

Once the *rule of life* is in final draft form, the whole church community may be called together to listen to a reading. This could happen in the fall of Year Two. At this meeting, invite people to offer written or verbal suggestions for improvements. The leaders work these changes into the *rule of life* and present the *rule of life* to the congregation for its approval and adoption.

At the end of Year Two, upon acceptance, a quality printed copy of this *rule of life* could be sent to every home, with a cover letter from the pastor or priest, and a brief study guide for practical use in homes, among families, and in small groups within the local church.

YEAR THREE. A local church is wise to gather people together regularly to discuss the practical implications of living according to the community *rule of life*, similar to the way a monastery will have regular chapter meetings. One possibility for introducing the *rule of life* to the people is simply to read sections of the rule during corporate worship each week, as part of the community sharing time. Potential new ministries and missions are to be evaluated according to the community *rule of life*.

Annual performance reviews of staff and leaders may also be based upon how staff and leaders have assisted the congregation in living according to the *rule of life*. I currently evaluate my performance as a pastor according to our mission statement. If we had a *rule of life* at Community Presbyterian Church, I would evaluate all I do as a pastor from this congregational guidebook. Pastors, elders, and deacons may consider renaming various ministries within the life of the church to better match the language and focus of *the rule of life*. Several years ago, we changed our Fellowship Elder position to become the Hospitality Elder, based upon *The Rule of St. Benedict*; and we also changed our Adult Discipleship Elder position to become the Spiritual Formation Elder. When the *rule of life* is taken seriously as a congregational guidebook, it becomes a living document, guiding the ministry, mission, and life together in the community of Christ.

In addition, during Year Three, leaders may begin to implement, in the weekly life of the local church, the paths of Christian formation as described above. This implementation may find a wide variety of forms and approaches depending upon the style and giftedness of the local church. At regular leadership meetings, ask evaluation questions about how the congregation is "progressing in this way of life and faith."

A more structured approach to implementation in Year Three may include the following schedule: in January–February, work on "Benedictine Essentials for Spiritual Formation." In March–April, follow "The Path of Prayer." In May–June, walk together along "The Path of Spiritual Guidance" by discussing ways to better mentor people in the congregation. In July–August, study "The Path of Ordinary Spirituality," and encourage members of the congregation to "practice the presence of God" in their everyday lives through the summer months. In September–October, journey along "The Path of *Lectio Divina*," implementing new approaches to sacred study of Scripture within the congregation. In November–December, evaluate how well you are welcoming others on "The Path of Hospitality."

With a community *rule of life* in place within the local church, members and church leaders will have a better way of journeying together as pilgrims of our Lord. In this way, the people of God will be equipped, empowered, and encouraged to "stand at the crossroads and look; ask for the ancient paths" (Jer. 6:16a), and walk together by faith, hope, and love, with Christ as their guide.

TAKING STEPS
INTO CHRISTIAN FORMATION
from Chapter Ten

- Ask three of your closest friends to take initial steps into Christian formation with you. Begin to pray together, learn to listen to Scripture together, and serve others together by putting into practice what you've learned from Christ.

- If you serve in the leadership of a local church, consider putting into action the "Three-Year Guide to Writing a *Rule of Life* for a Local Congregation." Call other church leaders together to study *Ancient Paths* and tailor this guide to best fit your setting for Christian formation.

- For those who are not involved in the leadership of a local church, consider writing a *rule of life* for your personal life, as well as for the lives of members of your family. Use the same outline presented in the "guide to writing a *rule of life*" but personalize it to fit your schedule and situation in life.

CHAPTER 11

User's Guide to Going on a Monastic Retreat

During a weeklong retreat to the Trappist monastery near Conyers Georgia, I met an old monk one night after Compline. Through a toothless grin he whispered to me, "You would have made such a great monk!" Though his comment was quite a compliment, it unsettled me a little. That night in bed, in the darkness of the monastic retreat center, I tried to picture what it would be like to actually become a white-haired, elderly monk after having lived the next fifty years of my life in the same monastery. I could not see the picture very clearly. Most of us nonmonks have a hard time imagining what life is really like within the monastic cloister, even for a weekend.

What does a monastic retreat look like? Come with me to see! After driving for several hours along freeways, state highways, and country lanes, I arrive at the guesthouse, receive my room assignment, and unpack my few belongings. What next? Look around the room. Notice how simple it is: a single well-made bed, a wooden desk, a wardrobe, a reading chair, and a lamp. On the wall, I notice a crucifix and an icon of some saint. Look out the window. The sunset casts an amber glow upon the willow tree by the lake. Hear the bells tolling. They are inviting us to come into the place of prayer, into the sanctuary, to join the Brothers for Vespers. There is no requirement. I can stay in my room if I prefer.

Or I could go out for an evening walk along the lakeside and enjoy the golden glow of the ending of another day. Why am I here? What has drawn me away to this place? A hunger and thirst for God. Nothing more; nothing less.

In the desk drawer I find a schedule outlining the monastic day, including mealtimes and hours for the Divine Office, the set times of daily prayer. I notice that Vespers happens daily at 5:30 PM. I look at my watch and see it is 5:29. Hurry! Heading out, I quickly walk across the courtyard to the church and take a place in the back just as Vespers begins. "O God, come to my assistance; O Lord, make haste to help me." The monks begin their evening chant. Already, I begin to sense a relaxing of the muscles around my neck. An unexplained drowsiness comes over me as the monks continue singing the evening psalms. The words of these prayers seem to wash over me like waves washing up on a stony shore. Then a robed monk reads a short lesson from the Bible. After the lesson, he sits down and a veil of silence settles upon the monks. This silence lasts much longer than expected. I look at my watch as the silent minutes slowly tick past. I cannot remember the last time I sat in silence for five minutes in a room full of other adults. I nod off into a semisleepy state, only to wake up to the words of the Lord's Prayer, "and lead us not into temptation." My mind has been reflecting upon the seductions faced over the past weeks. A sense of inner regret seeps into my spirit as the monks shuffle out. Vespers is over. As I step out of the pew in the back of the church, I find myself bowing before God and firing off a quick prayer of thanks. I walk out into the fresh evening air, feeling lighter and newer than I've felt in a long time.

As I head back to my room, leaping up flights of stairs two steps at a time, a little voice within wonders: *Why the hurry?* As I stand there on the landing, I have no idea why I'm hurrying up those stairs—just a habit of life, I suppose. I begin to walk slowly up the stairwell, one step at a time, and my mind and heart begin to enter into a whole new rhythm of life, a gentler, slower, more attentive approach to life with God.

Since 1986, I have retreated to monasteries for times of rest and renewal. These retreats have included Benedictine and Trappist monasteries across the country: St. Placid Benedictine Priory in Lacey, Washington; Mount Angel Benedictine Abbey in Mount Angel, Oregon; Our Lady of Guadalupe Trappist Abbey near Lafayette, Oregon; Christ in the Desert Benedictine Abbey near Abiquiu, New Mexico; Prince of Peace Benedictine Abbey near Oceanside, California; Gethsemani Trappist Abbey near Bardstown, Kentucky; and Monastery of the Holy Spirit Trappist Abbey near Conyers, Georgia.

My retreat habits have changed over the years. For the first few years, I went away to a monastery for a full week. Then I shifted to several weekend retreats per year, often in the spring and fall. For a few years, I made day retreats to a monastery two hours away, arriving at ten in the morning and leaving after Vespers, at six in the evening. Currently, I make a three-day retreat once a year at Mount Angel Benedictine Abbey, where I have been a Benedictine Oblate since February of 2006.

Hearing about these various monastic experiences, people often ask me questions about monastic retreats: Why retreat to a monastery? Where can we find a monastic retreat center nearby? What should we do upon arrival? What benefit might I receive from making a monastic retreat? This essay is written in part to answer such questions. The real purpose of this essay, though, is to encourage pilgrims of faith to begin walking the paths of Christian formation as expressed in *The Rule of St. Benedict*, through immersion in a monastic retreat setting.

FINDING A MONASTIC RETREAT CENTER

There was a time in the late medieval era of church history when one could find a monastery within a day's ride on horseback anywhere in Europe. Though the numbers of monasteries have declined over the past two hundred years, monasteries are still more prevalent and proximate than people realize. In order to find a monastery nearest your home, check out the listings of monasteries in such resources as your local Catholic diocese, the yellow pages in a metropolitan area phone book, or go online at www.osb.org and look up the listing of Benedictine monasteries. Most of my retreats to monasteries have involved driving two to four hours away from my home. I have found that this time alone in the car has helped me shift gears away from the many distractions and demands behind me, and prepared my mind and heart for the days ahead in a completely different rhythm and way of life.

I have written in this book about Benedictine spirituality as practiced at monasteries based in *The Rule of St. Benedict*, including Benedictine, Cistercian, and Trappist monasteries. Yet there are dozens of monastic orders who offer retreat facilities for guests: Franciscan, Dominican, Carmelite, and Claretian monastic orders among others. Websites and listings showing regional locations of retreat centers are readily available, and these include phone numbers and details regarding booking a retreat.

THE HEART OF A MONASTIC RETREAT

Often when Jesus went on pilgrimage to Jerusalem, he lodged in Bethany, in the home of Martha. On one of these annual visits to Jerusalem, "as Jesus and his disciples were on their way," they came again to Bethany to the home of Martha. "She had a sister called Mary, who sat at the Lord's feet listening to what he said" (Lk. 10:38–39). Disregarding the customary gender roles of her day, Mary had the audacity to spend time with the men, sitting at Jesus' feet "listening to what he said." Martha was not pleased with her sister's decision, for she "was distracted by all the preparations that had to be made" (Lk. 10:40a). Martha called Jesus away from the guests to lodge a complaint with him against her sister: "Lord, don't you care that my sister has left me to do the work by myself? Tell her to help me!" (Lk. 10:40b). Jesus then offered Martha a new way of looking at life. The words Jesus spoke to Martha continue to echo into our time and speak to all who would come after Martha, all who are distracted by "all the preparations that have to be made." Jesus spoke tenderly to Martha. "Martha, Martha, . . . you are worried and upset about many things, but only one thing is needed. Mary has chosen what is better, and it will not be taken away from her" (Lk. 10:41–42).

Since the early church, Christians have looked upon the domestic life in Bethany as recorded in the Gospel of Luke and have noticed a pattern for our daily living that involves a balancing of Martha and Mary—symbolizing the active life and the contemplative life. The Greek language offers two words for time: *kronos*, or clock-ticking time, and *kairos*, or God-present time. *Kronos* time may be viewed as "Martha time," with ticking timers on ovens telling you when the bread is done baking. *Kronos* time wears an apron and measures life by minutes and seconds. Martha time determines who we are by what we do.

Kairos time, or "Mary time," pays attention to God's presence, like Mary sitting at Jesus' feet. Less mindful of past regrets and future worries, "Mary time" lives in the present moment, basking in the rays of eternal sunshine streaming from God's presence. *Kairos* wears a prayer shawl and tells us that our lives are meant to be enjoyed in intimate relationship with God. Mary time reminds us that we are human *beings*, not human *doings*.

Jesus reveals to us a mature pattern for life that includes active involvement in the daily *kronos* time with others as well as retreat and withdrawal into the place of solitude to spend quality *kairos* time alone with God. Jesus commissioned his followers to go out into the villages and towns and actively invest themselves in the lives of needy people. When his followers returned from their mission and gathered around Jesus, they reported to him all they had done and taught. "Then, because so many people were coming and going that they did not even have a chance to eat, he said to them, 'Come with me by yourselves to a quiet place and get some rest'" (Mk. 6:31).

A monastic retreat takes us away from the "coming and going" of the many people who make demands upon our lives, and allows us to "get some rest," because we have been willing to come away in solitude to be with Christ at "a quiet place." Spiritual burnout presents a regular threat to anyone who works with people: pastors, ministers, teachers, nurses, doctors, and other people-oriented professionals. No matter how hard we may try to maintain a clinical distance with professional clients, people's needs weigh upon our lives, and we can "become weary in doing good" (see Gal. 6:9). In ministry, pastors willingly lay down their lives for people, seeking to teach, exhort, encourage, and build others up in Christ, yet they often fail to renew themselves inwardly during months and months of ministry. In the regular times away from the distractions of daily life and the professional demands of work, God offers us the gift of refreshment—the restoration of our soul (see Ps. 23:3).

Jesus often withdrew from the crowds to spend *kairos* time alone with God in prayer. He invites his followers to do the same. A monastic retreat calls us to come away from the distractions and preparations that have to be made, and spend some "Mary time" in silence, listening to the voice of Christ. "With joy you will draw water from the wells of salvation" (Isa. 12:3). We get away from the many distractions, the anxieties, and the worries of daily activities in order to sit by the well in the presence of God and draw water to quench our thirst.

WAYS TO ENJOY A MONASTIC RETREAT

When people ask me what to do while on retreat at a monastery, the quick answer to that question is not *do* anything. Just *be* with God. Nobody hands out any awards for super spirituality to people going on retreats at monasteries. With that basic perspective in mind, I offer the following five ways to enjoy a few days of retreat at a monastery. Take these as open invitations to come away to refresh your body, mind, and soul.

COME AWAY. Jesus invites followers to withdraw from the "coming and going" of all the people. On occasion, he calls us away from people in order to spend time alone with him. This seems strange at first, knowing that Christ calls us to go out into the world to personally enter people's lives with the Good News of the faith. But Jesus is very practical. He knows that spending time with people can be exhausting. He knows we need regular time alone with him in order to restore our souls. Only then will we be able to give ourselves freely to others and truly be a blessing to people. Out of the abundance we have received from Christ are we able to offer God's love to others. For this reason, we are wise to withdraw from people regularly. This means we also withdraw from phones, televisions, radios, and the Internet. We also withdraw from our spouse, children, family duties, and conversation with others we love. We are getting away from people in order to get closer to God. We treat ourselves to a monastic retreat by stepping away from the ordinary tasks and duties of home and stepping into God's presence through praying the Psalms, reading Scripture, and meditating within a monastic cloister.

ALONE WITH CHRIST. Solitude is not in vogue in our day. More than ever before, people are hurrying to get together, via car, phone, e-mail, chat rooms, or simply by walking among strangers at a shopping mall. People who enjoy time alone are looked upon as emotionally unstable, in need of therapy, or just a little weird. Why is solitude so frowned upon today? I believe it has to do with fear—a fear of facing my true inner self. The condition we know as "claustrophobia" comes from two words: *claustra*, Latin for enclosure or cloister, and *phobos*, or fear. Claustrophobia is the fear of being enclosed.

Cloister solitude may spark a fear of being suffocated, trapped, or imprisoned. This is one reason why a monastic retreat is such a wise practice. Inside the cloister, we begin to face our fears by surrounding ourselves with other contemplative brothers or sisters. In this safe, loving environment, we can begin to shed old ways and clothe ourselves in Christ's renewed way of life.

Solitude is more than merely being alone. The purpose is to be alone with God. According to the well-known American Trappist monk Thomas Merton,

> The solitary life makes sense only when it is centered entirely on the love of God. Without this, everything is triviality. Love of God

in Himself, for Himself, sought only in His will in total surrender. Anything but this in solitude is nausea and absurdity.

We withdraw from the busyness of life with others in order to draw closer to the love of God. Practically speaking, this means dealing with distractions. Once I get away into a monastic retreat, I realize my mind and heart is crowded with a noisy host of voices clamoring for attention. If I give in to these voices, I become, like Martha, "distracted by all the preparations" (see Lk. 10:40). I will always have lists of things to do, calls to return, tasks to perform, e-mail messages to answer. Mary's better portion is often lost. Retreat time involves sitting at the Lord's feet and listening to his teaching. A retreat welcomes us into the discipline of Christian meditation, in which we refocus our attention upon God alone by turning away from those other voices and truly listening to God.

LISTEN AT A LONELY PLACE. Active listening does not come naturally to most people. We are trained to speak during our first few years of life. We also need to be trained to listen—a process that can take years. In the school of listening, silence is our teacher. Again, listen to what Merton writes about this teacher in *Thoughts in Solitude*:

> My life is a listening, [God's] is a speaking. My salvation is to hear and respond. For this, my life must be silent. Hence, silence is my salvation. . . . Let me seek, then, the gift of silence . . . where everything I touch is turned into prayer.

A monastic retreat invites guests into this new way of prayer—the prayer of listening. Guests are invited to attend any of the monastic services throughout the day. Guests are provided with a liturgy of the service to follow along, either silently or to join vocally as they choose. Though the times for the daily Divine Office vary from place to place, the following schedule is common: Vigils—4:15 AM; Lauds—6:30 AM; Mass—7:30 AM; Day Hour—12:00 noon; Vespers—5:30 PM; Compline—7:30 PM.

In addition to the regular times of listening to the monks chant the Psalms at the Divine Office, I love to listen to quiet instrumental music to help turn my heart away from outside noise distractions and to focus my heart upon listening. Then, I open God's Word, especially the Psalms, and listen with my heart to God speaking through the psalmist. I also take time to journal, to write down what's on my heart, and what I sense is on God's heart. Rather than allow my heart's distractions to push their way onto center stage, I jot them down in a journal and commit them to God, who alone knows my heart.

LEISURE TO EAT. Guests are welcomed to join other guests for three meals a day at the retreat house dining room. Guests do not usually eat with the other monks. Several of the monks are assigned to the ministry of hospitality in the guesthouse and are seen at meal times serving the needs of the guests. Monasteries I have visited serve a hearty vegetarian fare, including homemade bread, and in the summer, homegrown vegetables. One daily meal, usually lunch, is a "silent meal." In the place of the usual socializing at meal times, guests listen to someone reading a book or hear a recorded lecture on some aspect of the life of faith.

Benedict not only encouraged reading during meal times, he instructed his monks to spend two to three hours a day enjoying time for prayerful reading. An integral part of a monastic retreat is immersion in prayerful reading. Different than other types of reading, sacred or prayerful reading focuses our whole attention upon God and what God is saying personally to us through this reading. A good book is food for the soul and spiritual nourishment. Every time I prepare to head off on a monastic retreat I scout out my bookshelves for books that I need to read, including nonfiction, fiction, and poetry.

The discipline of prayerful reading involves slow reading of the Bible and of other books that offer nourishment for a hungry soul. We read until we are touched by a certain phrase or sentence. We pause, taking time to meditate or think deeply about this truth. We ask God to shape our life with this truth—to feed our spirit with this holy food. Then, we continue our holy reading. Sometimes, I may write in a journal quotations or reflections on what I have learned from this time of holy reading.

Too often, people of faith only feed themselves once a week, during a community time of worship at Sunday worship service. If we only ate physical food once a week, we would not have the strength to live our lives as God intends for us to live. The same is true in the deeper realm of our spiritual lives. Christ invites us to draw away from the crowds in order to nourish our spirit with God's holy food.

REST AWHILE. Finally, during a monastic retreat, I get caught up on my doing nothing. I love the old Spanish proverb: "How beautiful it is to do nothing, then rest afterward!" On monastic retreats, I love heading out into the woods to talk with God and enjoy time together with God in nature. A slow-paced walk in the woods allows my inner life to drink in the goodness and beauty of God's creation. I find myself stopping often to observe the activity of some forest-dwelling creature: a copperhead snake in Georgia, a deer fawn in Oregon, blue-bellied lizards in New Mexico, or a gathering of crows in California have all offered me time to ponder the variety of God's creation.

Jesus told us to consider God's creation, including the ravens and the lilies (see Lk. 12:24, 27). The verb used in Greek for "consider" is *katanoeo*, or "observe thoroughly." Jesus calls us to use our minds to observe nature intently in order to fully study and understand such creatures as ravens. A monastic retreat opens up time to soak in God's creation and more carefully observe the work of the Creator through the wonder and beauty of nature. A monk friend once told me to go sit under a huge oak tree and just listen to the tree for an hour. At first, I thought the suggestion strange, but after that hour, my soul felt more rooted and quiet, more like the person mentioned in Psalm 1:2–3:

> But his delight is in the law of the LORD,
> and on his law he meditates day and night.
> He is like a tree planted by streams of water,
> which yields its fruit in season and whose leaf
> does not wither. Whatever he does prospers.

The other way I rest during a monastic retreat is by taking naps. Some adults feel guilty taking naps, as though a nap is a waste of valuable time that could be filled doing important tasks. Monastic retreats remind us that we are human *beings*, not human *doings*. Our lives are defined by who we are in God more than what we produce in a career. As the psalmist reminds us, "My soul finds rest in God alone; my salvation comes from him" (Ps. 62:1). Above the doorway leading into the Trappist Retreat House at Gethsemani Abbey in Kentucky you find the words GOD ALONE carved into the granite keystone. This simple reminder stuck with me long after I returned home into the active life. Thanks to regular monastic retreats, my soul's identity can rest in God alone, not in performance, accomplishments, or activities.

A few years ago, during an annual performance review with my supervisor, I was asked what single activity would improve my professional life. I told him that my life would deepen if I simply took up the discipline of spending one day a month in prayer and study. He said, "Let me see you write it into your calendar," and then waited until I had marked monastic retreats into my calendar for the next six months. He promised to ask each month how my retreats went.

Through the gift of monastic retreats, my inner life in Christ has been renewed, and I have grown deeper in my life of faith in God. When Christ calls us, he calls us not only to go out among people; he also calls us to draw away from people to a quiet place where we can truly rest in God alone. As spiritual beings, we need regular times of refreshment with God. I have discovered that the first day or two at a monastery are spent in an internal wrestling match between an old pattern of life and the new monastic rhythm of life. After forty-eight hours, I begin to settle into the monastic rhythm and find a true restoration going on deep within my soul. During these times, I have found my inner vision much clearer. My mind and heart seems less cluttered and less distracted. I am more attentive to God's "gentle whisper" (see 1 Kgs. 19:12) and more able to discern Christ's intent for my life and my future.

BRINGING THE MONASTERY HOME

After another retreat to Gethsemani Abbey, I stopped into a minute-mart in Bardstown to gas up before getting on the interstate. I recall the culture shock of hearing rap music blasting from a nearby car— seeing signs of excessive lifestyles all around me. There is something extraordinarily simple and sacred about time away at a monastery. Returning home can be quite a shock.

I have encouraged many friends to attempt such a monastic retreat and have been amused at their responses upon their return. One pastor could not get over the fact that most of the monks wore Reebok tennis shoes. His image of a monk included medieval footwear. What we wear on our feet has something to do with how we travel in this life. The best footwear provides comfort, support, and durability over many miles.

Here are three gifts anyone can bring home from a monastic retreat. First, come home refreshed and renewed in the comforting presence of Christ. Allow God to move into your daily life back home with regular times of rest and comfort. We easily get weary of daily tasks, even those that are for our good. A monastic retreat is meant to be a comforting time when we can lay our heads down and rest for a while in God's goodness. Each night, take "Mary time" to simply rest for a while in the presence of Christ.

Second, find a few other people in your daily life that will support you as you seek to implement something from those few days away at the monastery. We need loving accountability in our lives if we are truly going to grow in Christ. We were not meant to travel alone. Our pilgrimage is taken with others. Even if our close friends have never been to a monastery, they can still take an active interest in our times away, encouraging the regular refreshment that comes from this "Mary Time."

Finally, we can seek to change in ways that are lasting. In any new movement of the soul, there is always the danger of the "flash in the pan" approach to Christian formation. An impressive flare up of activity in the days immediately following a monastic retreat often end with a burnt smell in the air and little to show for our efforts. We are wise to implement what we can manage daily—plans that will endure through months and years. We must pray as we can, not as we imagine we should. Through the past two decades of monastic retreats, I have sought to add to my life little by little, step by step, allowing the Holy Spirit to transform my heart, my will, and my lifestyle incrementally. As we learn to walk together into Benedictine spirituality, we can expect that the unseen presence of Christ will come alongside us along the way, just as he did long ago on the Emmaus Road—joining us on our journey home.

TAKING STEPS
INTO CHRISTIAN FORMATION
from Chapter Eleven

- Consider going on a monastic retreat. First, find a monastic retreat center near your home and call up to check on available dates. Set a date and get away for a time for spiritual refreshment.
- Follow the five steps for "enjoying a monastic retreat" already listed.
- Bring something home with you from the monastery: possibly a new spiritual habit to put into your weekly schedule; or perhaps a book on spirituality you picked up at the monastic bookshop.
- Find a few other people in your daily life who are willing to support you as you try to implement the new ways of living you've learned from your time away at the monastery.

CHAPTER 12

A Year of Tools for Christian Formation

The following list is adapted from the *Rule*, chapter four. Benedict writes, "These, then are the tools of the spiritual craft. When we have used them without ceasing day and night and have returned them on judgment day, our wages will be the reward the Lord has promised" (RB, 4.75–76). You will find listed in this chapter a tool for every week of the year, along with a companion passage of Scripture and reference from the *Rule*. Try to implement these tools in your daily life, especially among the people in the local church where you worship as you seek to build these qualities of spirituality into your life as well as into those close to you in the family of faith.

If you are currently involved in a small group within your local congregation, consider practicing this list of tools and seeking practical ways to implement these tools in your daily life together over the period of one year. When you meet together with a few others for mutual encouragement and growth in the Christian life, you may find it helpful to employ such tools week by week and to ask questions of accountability connected to the use of each tool. For example:

- Name a time this past week when you turned toward someone who needed your love.

- Describe one way you have refrained from too much food, sleep, or laziness this past week.
- When was the last time you sat with a grieving person to listen to their heart?
- How have your responded recently to someone who injured you?
- What do you do when you find wrong thoughts entering your heart?
- Name a few ways you have treasured a life of purity this week.

These are the kind of accountability questions a small group of people can offer one another from Benedict's list of tools. Besides small group accountability, these tools might also offer a year's worth of sermon texts or studies in a Bible class within a local church. Another idea may be to post these tools on a prominent bulletin board, in the church newsletter, or on the church website homepage to emphasize the "tool of the week." Seek creative ways of encouraging the exercise of that tool within the community of faith each week for a whole year. In this way, a congregation may see a deepening of its life together in Christ through intentional Christian formation in the workshop of the Lord.

A YEAR OF TOOLS FOR SPIRITUAL FORMATION

JANUARY

1. Love God (Luke 10:27; RB, 4.1).
2. Love one another (John 13:34; RB, 4.2).
3. Uphold marriage and the sanctity of life (Hebrews 13:1–4; RB, 4.3–4).

4. Serve others with compassion (Ephesians 4:28–32; RB, 4.5–6).

5. Be honest (Mark 10:19; RB, 4.7).

FEBRUARY

1. Respect one another (1 Peter 2:17; RB, 4.8).

2. Practice the Golden Rule (Matthew 7:12; RB, 4.9).

3. Follow Christ (Matthew 16:24; RB, 4.10).

4. Learn to fast (Isaiah 58:6–7; 1 Corinthians 9:27; RB, 4.11–13).

MARCH

1. Help the poor (Matthew 25:36; RB, 4.14–15).

2. Care for the sick (Matthew 25:36; RB, 4.16).

3. Comfort the grieving (2 Corinthians 1:3–4; RB, 4.17–19).

4. Live a Christlike lifestyle (Luke 4:5–8; Matthew 5:43–48; RB, 4.20).

APRIL

1. Love Christ above all else (2 Corinthians 5:14; RB, 4.21).

2. Deal daily with anger (Ephesians 4:26; 1 Corinthians 13:5; RB, 4.22–23).

3. Strive for purity of heart (Matthew 5:8; 1 Corinthians 13:6; RB, 4.24).

4. Practice peacemaking (Matthew 5:9; RB, 4.25).

MAY

1. Offer hospitality from the heart (Romans 12:13; RB, 4.26).

2. Live a life of truth (Ephesians 4:15; RB, 4.27–28).

3. Express kindness to others (1 Thessalonians 5:15; 1 Peter 3:9; RB, 4.29).

4. Forbear grievances (Matthew 5:39; Colossians 3:13; RB, 4.30).

5. Love your enemies (Matthew 5:44; Luke 6:27; RB, 4.31).

JUNE

1. Bless others, especially angry, hurting people (Romans 12:14; RB, 4.32).

2. Endure hardships with patience (1 Peter 2:20–21; Matthew 5:10; RB, 4.33).

3. Live a life of humility (1 Peter 5:6; RB, 4.34).

4. Live with moderation (Titus 1:7–8; RB, 4.35–37).

JULY

1. Be zealous and keep spiritual fervor (Romans 12:11; Galatians 6:9; RB, 4.38).

2. Encourage others (1 Thessalonians 5:11; RB, 4.39–40).

3. Hope in God alone (Psalm 62:1; RB, 4.41).

4. Experience God's goodness (Psalm 16; RB, 4.42).

5. Take responsibility for shortcomings (Psalm 51; RB, 4.43).

AUGUST

1. Maintain an eternal perspective (2 Corinthians 4:16–18; RB, 4.44–46).

2. Die daily (1 Corinthians 15:31; RB, 4.47).

3. Be watchful (Matthew 26:41; RB, 4.48–49).

4. Train our thoughts in godliness (Psalm 139; Philippians 4:8; RB, 4.50).

5. Use our words to build up others in love (Ephesians 4:29; RB, 4.51–52).

SEPTEMBER

1. Learn to laugh (Psalm 126; RB, 4.53–54).

2. Listen to God (Ecclesiastes 5:1–2; John 10:27; RB, 4.55).

3. Pray daily (1 Thessalonians 5:17; RB, 4.56).

4. Confess our sins to God (Psalm 32; RB, 4.57–58).

OCTOBER

1. Delay gratification (Galatians 5:16; RB, 4.59–60).

2. Practice mutual submission (Ephesians 5:21–33; RB, 4.61).

3. Grow in holiness (Romans 12:1–2; RB, 4.62).

4. Live by God's commandments daily (Matthew 7:24–25;
   RB, 4.63).

NOVEMBER

1. Treasure sexual purity (Hebrews 13:4; RB, 4.64).

2. Live with charity and contentment (Philippians 1:9, 4:12;
   RB, 4.65–66).

3. Live in love (1 Corinthians 13:4–8; RB, 4:67–69).

4. Look after widows and orphans (James 1:27; RB, 4.70).

DECEMBER

1. Love children (James 1:27; Ephesians 6:4; RB, 4.71).

2. Pray for others, especially those who mistreat you
   (Luke 6:27–28; RB, 4.72).

3. Sleep in peace (Psalm 4:8; Ephesians 4:26; RB, 4.73).

4. Hope in God's mercy (Hebrews 10:23; James 2:13;
   RB, 4.74).

TAKING STEPS
INTO CHRISTIAN FORMATION
from Chapter Twelve

- Copy the above list and put it up in a visible place in your home, such as on your refrigerator door.

- Try to implement one tool a week from this list for the period of one year. Ask yourself each week, *How can I best live out this tool today?*

- Ask God for wisdom and guidance in building these virtues and tools into your daily life.

- If you are involved in leadership in a local church, see about implementing these tools in the life of the whole congregation, in Bible study groups, sermons, church bulletin boards, newsletters, or even on the church website.

- Ask a few close friends to go through the list with you. Star those tools that stand out. Put a question mark by those tools that seem strange or out of reach. Talk with your friends about your stars and questions marks. Encourage each other to put these tools into practice.

Guidance on Ancient Paths

> All along my pilgrim journey, Savior, let me walk with Thee. . . .
>
> Gladly will I toil and suffer, only let me walk with Thee.
>
> Lead me through the vale of shadows, bear me o'er life's fitful sea;
>
> Then the gate of life eternal may I enter, Lord with thee.
>
> —FANNY CROSBY

Blind hymn writer Fanny Crosby wrote in her journal about how she came to compose the preceding hymn, "Close to Thee": "Toward the close of a day in the year 1874, I was sitting in my room thinking of the nearness of God through Christ as the constant companion of my pilgrim journey." Through Christ as the constant companion of our pilgrim journey, we can expect to make progress in the lifelong goal of spiritual maturity. Like Fanny Crosby, we walk by faith not by sight. We need a guide along the way if we are truly to grow into maturity in God.

The journey of Christian formation is not primarily our work, but rather a gracious gift from God. Jesus told his disciples, "You did not choose me, but I chose you and appointed you to go and bear fruit—fruit that will last" (Jn. 15:16a). Christ has chosen us and appointed us to follow him along the pilgrim way of fruitful living. Throughout this writing, I've retraced steps of Benedictine spirituality along ancient paths. *The Rule of St. Benedict* has been our guidebook, chapter by chapter—a source for Christian formation in the twenty-first century. Benedictine spirituality provides principles and well-tested practices for Christian formation, especially within the setting of a local church community. Benedict closes the *Rule* just as he began, with his favorite image, that of walking together with Christ:

> Are you hastening toward your heavenly home? Then with Christ's help, keep this little rule that we have written for beginners. After that, you can set out for the loftier summits of the teaching and virtues we mentioned above, and under God's protection you will reach them. Amen. (RB, 73.8–9)

In these closing words, we see a clear vision for spiritual growth: pilgrims of Christ traveling together as a community toward our heavenly home with God. We walk with Christ's help; strengthened step-by-step through the grace of God. Along the way, we need basic instructions to help us follow the path of Christian formation. We walk together by faith, "prefer[ring] nothing whatever to Christ" (RB, 72.11), seeking to follow the Lord along well-traveled paths. As Tolkien wrote of life's journey,

> The Road goes ever on and on
> Down from the door where it began.
> Now far ahead the Road has gone,
> And I must follow, if I can,
> Pursuing it with eager feet,
> Until it joins some larger way
> Where many paths and errands meet.
> And whither then? I cannot say.

You may be wondering where this path of Benedictine spirituality may lead you. If you are involved in a local church, especially as a pastor or lay leader, you also may be wondering what would happen if you began to implement this Benedictine vision for Christian formation among the people you serve. As I've talked with people over the two decades since I first "met" Benedict, some have pulled me aside, expressing their concerns for my spiritual life, wondering if I've lost my wits or become some odd medieval monk-wannabe. I tell them what I've shared with you in these pages: along this road I've grown closer to Jesus Christ, received spiritual refreshment for my soul, and found wisdom and guidance to help build up Christ's people, the church. Along with countless other fellow-pilgrims along the way of Christ, "I must follow, if I can," pursuing this way "with eager feet." I'm aware there are other ways to live as a follower of Christ and many other approaches to formation within the local church. What this book offers you is a way of Christian formation that has been lived daily by individuals and communities of Christian pilgrims all around the world for fifteen centuries.

I invite you to join with me and with thousands of others who have opened "the door where it began." This journey begins by opening the ears of our heart: "Listen carefully . . . to the master's instructions and attend to them with the ear of your heart" (RB, prologue 1). As all hikers do once they've laced up their boots and put on their backpacks, let us step out upon this road, the way of Benedictine formation, and discover the "inexpressible delight" of walking in "this way of life and in faith." Benedict set his sights upon the loftier summits of God's glory in eternal life with our Lord. Upon what have you set your sights? In these pages, we've not only looked back into history for guidance, but we've also looked ahead to new ways to journey together as pilgrims of the true king, Christ the Lord. "Far ahead the Road has gone" and we "must follow if we can." Though unfamiliar with the way ahead, we have a faithful guide to walk by our side.

One of the great gifts I've discovered since I began my Benedictine pilgrimage is the gift of support and encouragement from a faith community. This way of life is not a passing Christian fad that made the best-seller list last year but will be all but forgotten next year. There are many approaches to church growth and to the Christian spiritual life. Some are based upon clear principles from Scripture, and others are based upon mass-marketing, corporate management skills, or the entertainment industry. Meanwhile, the Benedictine monks continue to pray the Psalms, to meditate upon Scripture, and to daily intercede for the church and for the world.

The Benedictine way of life begun fifteen centuries ago, as described with such wisdom, modesty, and balance in the *Rule*, is still guiding the daily spiritual lives of countless believers living in Christian communities all around the world. There will come a new day down the road when all pilgrims will meet at last, and "join some larger way where many paths and errands meet." Until that glorious day, Christ calls us to follow him, and to learn to walk together by faith, hope, and love along the way he sets before us. This book was written to encourage you to discover anew paths of Christian formation. Just as Benedict and his community of faith discovered how to grow together in their life with Christ in the early sixth century, so fifteen centuries later, may a whole new generation of pilgrims of Christ walk in the ancient way, and in so doing, bring Christ's renewal and peace to our world in this new century.

O God, the strength of all who trust in you,

be present with us as we pray;

and as we are weak, and can do nothing without you,

grant us always the help of your grace,

so that running in the path of your commands

our every deed and desire may please you.

We make our prayer through Christ our Lord.

May the peace of God, which passes all understanding,

be with us throughout this day.

And with all those we love. Amen.

ACKNOWLEDGMENTS

An arborist once told me that trees intertwine their root systems beneath our feet and form an interlocking community of trees we call a forest. In a similar manner, this book has been nourished by an interlocking root system of mentors, spiritual guides, friends, and family.

Thanks to Jon Sweeney, Robert Edmonson, and Paraclete Press for their support and editorial guidance in getting this book into print.

I am grateful for two Fuller Theological Seminary professors, my mentors and friends, Dr. James E. Bradley, professor of church history, and Dr. Richard Peace, professor of evangelism and spiritual formation.

Thanks also to my Fuller cohorts, who shared four years of doctoral studies with me in Christian spiritual formation: Steve, John, Eric, Frank, Fel, Peter, CP, Viola, Joyce, Miriam, Eric, Tom, John, Adrienne, and Jeff. What a gift of encouragement you've all been to my life.

I also express my heart gratitude to the loving people of Community Presbyterian Church, Cannon Beach, Oregon. You put Benedictine spirituality into action week after week, welcoming others "as Christ," as well as nurturing me and my family with your prayers, friendship, and love.

I also extend my gratitude to the many monks who have welcomed me during my many retreats and also to our circle of friends. As Dinah

Maria Mulock Craik once wrote of friends: "Oh, the comfort, the inexpressible comfort, of feeling safe with a person, having neither to weigh thoughts nor measure words, but pouring them all out, just as they are." We enjoy many such friends and are grateful for your love, and the "inexpressible comfort of feeling safe" with you.

Special thanks to Gladys Sawyer and to Jerry and Pam Railton, who welcomed me into their ocean-view homes for extended times of study and writing over the past four years.

Finally, I offer my love and gratitude to my family—for sweet years of life and love shared with you. Thanks to our grown kids, Jonathan and Christina, Stefan and Jessica, and Thomas, and most of all, my love and gratitude to my best friend and wife, Trina.

Twelve-Week Study Guide for Ancient Paths

The following study questions were written for small groups and lay leaders in the local church as a way to explore Benedictine guidance for Christian formation in a congregational setting. One possible format in which to use these questions is during the regularly scheduled meetings of the leaders of the church. Invite leaders to come thirty minutes earlier for a study of *Ancient Paths*. One leader is designated as the facilitator for the discussion. Prior to each month, each leader in the church will need to have read the material in that specific chapter of *Ancient Paths*. Over the period of a year, new approaches and foundations for ministry, especially the ministry of Christian formation, may be conceived and birthed through this monthly group study.

ANCIENT PATHS: A TWELVE-WEEK STUDY GUIDE

WEEK 1: WHICH WAY WILL WE GO?

1. What are some of your favorite pictures of the Christian faith from Scripture? How do you relate to pilgrimage or journey as a picture of faith? What journey stories in the Bible have helped you better understand the Christian faith? Share a story from your own journey of faith. Read aloud some of the pilgrimage Bible passages mentioned in the introduction.

2. What are some of your views of monasticism? Prior to reading *Ancient Paths*, how much have you known about Benedictine monasticism? How surprising is it to you to be studying monasticism as a guidebook for Christian formation in the local church?

3. Name some alternative lifestyles commonly found in our culture today. Of the three alternative ways of living in the introduction, which is most prevalent in this community: Life-alone? Life-without-rules? Life-on-the-move? Which is most dangerous in the church?

4. How does Benedict's approach to formation differ from these alternatives? What is the place of vow-making and vow-keeping in society today? What is the place of vow-making in the local church? If you are a member of a local congregation, what promises or commitments did you make when you joined? What might be the place of sacred vows and promises in the way we welcome new members?

WEEK 2: HOW BENEDICT TRANSFORMED THE WORLD

1. What stands out to you in Benedict's story? What were some of the major troubles in society in Benedict's time? Name some of the challenges Benedict faced in his life. What kind of a person was Benedict? What kind of a spiritual leader was he?

2. What was the lasting legacy of Benedictine monasticism upon Europe in the medieval period? How can we be a positive influence in our world today? Consider the spread of Christianity across Europe in medieval times through Benedictine missionaries, including through the Cluniac and Cistercian

movements. How is Christianity being spread today? How is our church involved in the spread of the gospel of Christ?

3. What was unique about Benedict's approach to Christian formation? How did Benedict design his faith community? How does this design compare with the approach to Christian formation in the church today?

4. "Life together under vows, life together under a communal *Rule*, and life together under wise spiritual leadership." How do these three Benedictine approaches to Christian formation provide perspective on Christian living in our time?

WEEK 3: BENEDICTINE ESSENTIALS FOR THE JOURNEY

1. What essential tools are you currently using for spiritual formation in your life? What tools are used within your local congregation? Who decides what is essential for formation in the local church?

2. The longest chapter in the *Rule* is Benedict's chapter on humility. How is this virtue being promoted among members of the body of Christ today? How would Benedict's twelve steps of humility improve the life of the church today?

3. Discuss the Benedictine "essentials" brought up in chapter two and evaluate each of these according to how it may help you grow in your spiritual life with Christ. Write below any ideas or brainstorms that come to you about:

   - Spiritual Leadership
   - Shared Wisdom
   - Tools for Spiritual Formation
   - Obedience
   - Twelve Steps into Humility

WEEK 4: THE PATH OF COMMUNAL PRAYER

1. Who taught you to pray and when did you first begin praying? What does this say about how we learn to pray? Would you describe yourself as a novice or an expert when it comes to prayer? What is the essence of prayer?

2. What times of the day do you tend to pray? Is there a better time during the day or night to pray? What makes it better for you? How often do people meet to pray together in your local church? What do you think of Benedict's plan for adding more structured time for praying together?

3. What has been your experience in praying the Psalms? How are the Psalms utilized in the prayer life of your local church? What plans or structures have you found helpful in learning to pray the Psalms?

4. What role does the church calendar play in spiritual formation in your local church? Does your local church currently have a prayer room, prayer groups, prayer cards, and/or regular prayer events through the church year? How central is prayer and worship to the life of your congregation?

WEEK 5: THE PATH OF SPIRITUAL GUIDANCE

1. What are some of your first responses when you read about the path of spiritual guidance offered in chapter four? What role, if any, do you currently play in offering spiritual guidance to others?

2. How are leaders chosen in your local church? How are they trained? What good ideas from this chapter are potential ways of improving the leadership of the church?

3. What type of training or instruction are lay leaders given through the year to help develop their ability to offer people spiritual care? What do you think of the Benedictine guidance for such instruction offered in this chapter? What is the role of admonition in the local church? Why is this ministry often neglected in congregational life? Where have you experienced admonition? How might this ministry be improved in this local church?

4. Define "spiritual direction" as described in this chapter. What metaphors for direction did you find helpful? What are some of the important tools for spiritual direction? How might a ministry of spiritual direction be initiated in your local church?

WEEK 6: THE PATH OF ORDINARY SPIRITUALITY

1. "Benedictine spirituality invites us to see all of life as sacred." How do you see life? Benedict considered all vessels and tools in the monastery as "sacred vessels of the altar." How might this approach to material objects within a local church change the way we handle possessions in the church?

2. What place do children have within the ministry of the local church? Who is the most playful person you know in your local church? What do you like most about this person? How can we become more childlike as Jesus instructed?

3. What is the place for kitchen service, food service, meal preparation, and such domestic tasks within the local church? Who is in charge of these tasks? How are these people selected? How are they trained? What qualifications are there for those in charge of food in a church?

4. Who is in charge of the building and grounds of the church? Who owns the church building and everything in it? How is this responsibility shared among members of the congregation? How willing are people to share of their material possessions—their finances, material goods, food, clothing, and their own physical labor?

WEEK 7: THE PATH OF *LECTIO DIVINA*

1. How often do you study the Scripture together with other believers? Do the current spiritual leaders of the church study Scripture together? What do you find most rewarding about your own personal habit of studying Scripture?

2. Who taught you to read? What were some of the favorite books you read growing up? What are you reading at this time? How would you describe your reading diet?

3. What roles do silence and solitude play in your spiritual life as a person? What role do these have in the life of the local church? How might these be integrated into various settings within the local church? What good might come from these two classic spiritual disciplines?

4. Describe sacred study of Scripture. What are the various stages of sacred study of Scripture mentioned in chapter six? Does this church currently have any small groups that regularly practice this approach to Scripture? How might such a spiritual discipline be brought into the regular life of this congregation? What did you find most helpful about chapter six?

WEEK 8: THE PATH OF HOSPITALITY

1. "All guests who present themselves are to be welcomed as Christ, for he himself will say: *I was a stranger and you welcomed me* (Matt. 25:35)" (RB, 53.1). What would happen if your church put this sentence into practice every week?

2. Define hospitality. How is this ministry currently being practiced in the local church? How welcoming is this church to guests, strangers, out-of-towners, and spiritual seekers? How might we improve upon the way we welcome others?

3. What are some practical ways of practicing hospitality? What are some of the challenges involved in walking on the path of hospitality?

4. What are some longer strides in practicing hospitality? How can this spiritual path change the world? What are some examples you can give of people who were world-change agents through the ministry of Christ-centered hospitality?

WEEK 9: HOW BENEDICT IS STILL TRANSFORMING THE WORLD

1. How are people brought into the spiritual life and the intentional community of your church today? How are you currently caring for newcomers and supporting new members? How might this be improved, based upon Benedict's vision and vows?

2. Name some areas in contemporary society where you see instability. What help might the "way of stability in community" offer to people in today's world? How might this vow be implemented in the church?

3. Name some specific problems caused by infidelity, not only in marriages, but also in other arenas of life. What help might the "way of fidelity in community" offer to people in today's world? How might this vow be implemented in the church today?

4. What would happen in our world today if obedience was completely neglected? What help might the "way of obedience in community" offer to people in today's world? How might this vow be implemented in your local church?

WEEK 10: FIVE CASE STUDIES OF CHRISTIAN FORMATION

1. Of the five examples offered from the twentieth century, which story most interested you and informed you regarding Christian formation in community? What can be learned from these five lists of lessons that might deepen the life of the church in spiritual formation?

2. Consider purchasing a copy of Bonhoeffer's *Life Together* and spending the next few months slowly studying this excellent guide to Christian formation in community.

3. Do you know anyone who has visited or become familiar with any of these movements? If anyone has made a visit or pilgrimage to Iona, Scotland; to Lindisfarne or Northumbria, England; or to Taizé, France, share your experience with the group. What is the role today of making such sacred pilgrimages?

4. What do you find helpful and inspiring in the twelve marks of "new monasticism"? Which of these twelve would you like to see become a part of your life or the life of your local church? What steps in the journey into congregational

formation are you currently taking in your local church? What steps might you take together in the future?

WEEK 11: A GUIDE FOR CHRISTIAN FORMATION IN A LOCAL CHURCH

1. What has been your experience, if any, in long-range planning as a congregation? Has the local church in which you are active ever done a "mission study" or experienced a yearlong study of church growth?

2. What was your response when you first read "A Guide for Christian Formation in a Local Church" in chapter ten? Recognizing that this is offered only as a sample outline for developing a plan for Christian formation in a local church, what in this outline may be applicable to your setting? Describe a few places in the local church where the "first steps" from Benedict's prologue (praying together, listening to Scripture together, serving others together) are already being taken.

3. What are some of your thoughts about the value of a *rule of life* in a community of faith such as a local church? Which of the case study examples of a *rule of life* seems best suited for your situation?

4. From *Ancient Paths*, what has been most helpful to you as a guide for your personal life of faith? What do you think would be most helpful as a guide for Christian formation within the local church?

WEEK 12: A YEAR OF TOOLS FOR SPIRITUAL FORMATION

1. What are some of your most commonly used tools in your home? Describe a time when you didn't have the right tool for a job. How did you respond?

2. Read through the list of tools again. How do you respond to this list? Now consider spreading out this list across a whole year, focusing upon one tool per week. How does that change the way you look at the list?

3. Please go through the list one more time to put a star next to your top five tools (those that seem to jump up off the page). Put a question mark next to the five tools that you are unsure of how they would be practiced. Share with others one of your stars and one of your question marks.

4. When looking over the various ideas for putting these tools to use in a local church, which idea seems to make good sense to you? Write out other ideas for possible action that were not listed.

vii   *Like all monasteries*   For ease of reference throughout, *The Rule of St. Benedict* will be referred to as the *Rule* or RB, with numerical chapter and verse references provided for citations as appropriate. Unless otherwise noted, all quotations from the *Rule* are from Timothy Fry, ed., *RB 1980: The Rule of St. Benedict in English* (Collegeville, MN: Liturgical Press, 1982).

xi   *This is what the LORD says:*   All Scripture quotations are from the *Holy Bible, New International Version* (Grand Rapids, MI: Zondervan, 1984).

xi   *Thou my everlasting portion,*   "Close to Thee," by Fanny J. Crosby, first published in *Songs of Grace and Glory*, W.F. Sherwin and S.J. Vail, eds. (New York: Horace Waters & Sons, 1874). Though blind from early childhood, Fanny Crosby wrote more than six thousand hymns in her lifetime, including "Close to Thee," a hymn that employs the metaphor of faith as a lifelong spiritual journey with Christ.

xvi   *According to a Gallup poll*   See www.gallup.com; poll 27877 and poll 1690 accessed June 9, 2008).

xvii   *The international community of Benedictine Oblates*   When I became a Benedictine Oblate in February 2006, I made a lifelong promise to "dedicate myself to the service of God and humanity according to *The Rule of Saint Benedict* in so far as my state in life permits." Brother Benet Tvedten, OSB, asks in his book *How to Be a Monastic and Not Leave Your Day Job*, "Is the Rule of St. Benedict really relevant for people living in the twenty-first century? Apparently it is. Benedictinism is common ground for everyone. There are in the world an estimated 24,155 Oblates of St. Benedict" (Brewster, MA: Paraclete Press, 2006), 109. For more information on the Benedictine family of believers, including detailed information about the Benedictine Oblate way of life, see the Order of Saint Benedict website at www.osb.org.

5   *During his boyhood [Benedict]*   Gregory the Great, *Life and Miracles of St. Benedict*, trans. Odo J. Zimmerman, OSB (Collegeville, MN: Liturgical Press, 1984), 1–2.

5   *Why? Not because he was doing poorly*   Jean Leclercq, OSB, *The Love of Learning and the Desire for God*, trans. Catharine Misrahi (New York: Fordham University Press, 1974), 14–15.

6   *Almost half-way between*   Ildephonsus Herwegen, OSB, *St. Benedict: A Character Study*, trans. Dom Peter Nugent, OSB (London: Herder Books, 1924), 58.

7   *While he had a high regard*   Most historians agree that Benedict never entered the priesthood. The best evidence of his status as a lay brother comes from Benedict's earliest biographer, Gregory the Great, who never mentions Benedict's ordination or service as a priest. Also, Benedict's style of writing belies that of a lay person—someone more interested in the practical aspects of communal living than the ecclesiastical vocation of a priest. See Kenneth Scott Latourette, *A History of Christianity: Vol I, Beginnings to 1500* (New York: Harper & Row, 1975), 333.

7   *"To the modern reader,*   Timothy Fry, Timothy Horner, and Imogene Baker, eds., *RB 1980: The Rule of St. Benedict in Latin and English with Notes* (Collegeville, MN: Liturgical Press, 1981), 410–11. Hereafter this book will be called *RB 1980*.

8   *"Benedictine monasticism spread slowly*   W.H.C. Frend, *The Rise of Christianity* (Philadelphia: Fortress Press, 1985), 883.

8   *"At Canterbury Augustine began*   Latourette, *A History of Christianity*, 346.

9   *"The wide dissemination*   Edwin Mullins, *Cluny: In Search of God's Lost Empire* (New York: BlueBridge, 2006), 24.

9   *The oldest surviving copy*   Christopher Brooke, *The Age of the Cloister: The Story of Monastic Life in the Middle Ages* (Mahwah, NJ: HiddenSpring, 2003), 59.

9   *"It remains a faithful copy*   Brooke, *The Age of the Cloister*, 59. In September 2008, I was privileged to spend three hours at the Stiftsbibliothek medieval library in St. Gallen, Switzerland, studying this rare manuscript, Codex Sangallensis 914, page by page, reading this rare ninth-century book with gloved hands. In the digital age, this manuscript is now available to any with computer access through photographic imaging. See www.cesg.unifr.ch/en (accessed October 13, 2008).

10 *"Louis made Benedict*   Latourette, *A History of Christianity*, 358.

10 *"Cluny's abbots,"*   Mullins, *Cluny*, 1.

10 *By the end of the twelfth century,*   Mullins, *Cluny*, 145.

14 *Though several monastic hospitals in London*   See www.nhshistory.net/voluntary_hospitals.htm (accessed April 28, 2010).

14 *The phrase* ora et labora,   While the phrase *ora et labora*, or "pray and work," does not appear in the *Rule*, in chapter 48 Benedict speaks of work within the monastery, including the work of prayer, study of Scripture, and manual labor.

15 *In those distant days*   Mullins, *Cluny*, 7.

15 *Uniting the vows of poverty*   Frend, *The Rise of Christianity*, 883.

22 *In his commentary on the* Rule,   Terrence G. Kardong, osb, *Benedict's Rule: A Translation and Commentary* (Collegeville, MN: Liturgical Press, 1996), 75.

28 *Instead of recovery from substance addiction,*   I am indebted to J. Keith Miller, *A Hunger for Healing: The Twelve Steps as a Classic Model for Christian Spiritual Growth* (New York: HarperCollins, 1991), for his insightful book on the twelve steps of AA as a practical approach to Christian spiritual maturity.

29 *According to Christian teachers,*   C.S. Lewis, *Mere Christianity* (London: Garden City Press, 1952), 96.

32 *"For a long moment we grasped*   Corrie Ten Boom, *Tramp for the Lord* (New York: Jove Books, 1978), 55.

34 *"Because, for three years*   Thomas Merton, trans., *The Wisdom of the Desert: Sayings from the Desert Fathers of the Fourth Century* (New York: New Directions, 1960), 39.

37 *"I divide the causes*   C.S. Lewis, *The Screwtape Letters* (New York: Macmillan, 1976), 50.

37 *"Flippancy builds up around*   Lewis, *The Screwtape Letters*, 52.

41 *Following Christ requires*   The imagery of "balconeers" and "travelers" comes from J.I. Packer in his book *Knowing God* (Downers Grove, IL: InterVarsity Press, 1973), 5.

42 *Jonah's prayer consisted*   Jonah's prayer includes quotations from Psalm 3:8, 11:4, 18:6, 30:3, 31:22, 42:7, 50:14, 50:23, 69:1–2, 77:11–12, 86:13, 88:6, 116:14, and 120:1.

42 *"During the winter season*   Benedict utilized the Roman system of hours for marking days and nights. The day hours were understood as the total sum of daylight in any given season divided by twelve. The night hours, similarly, were the total sum of darkness divided by twelve. Thus the Roman hour varied from forty-five to seventy-five minutes depending upon the season. The eighth hour for Benedict was around two in the morning. See Fry, *RB 1980*, 203.

46 *Benedict chose a variety*   In Benedict's chapters on morning prayers, he includes the following psalms as those for prayer in the morning hours: 5, 34, 51, 57, 63, 65, 67, 95, 98, 113, 118, 148, 149, and 150.

46 *The entire day received order*   Dietrich Bonhoeffer, *Psalms: The Prayerbook of the Bible* (Minneapolis: Augsburg, 1970), 64–65.

49 *As a contemporary discipline,*   Benedict follows the Latin Bible numbering of the Psalms, which varies in many places by one number from the Hebrew Bible numbering of the Psalms. This writing follows the common numbering system of the Psalms found in most contemporary English translations, such as the NRSV and the NIV, which are based upon the Hebrew Bible numbering.

53 *In* The Way of the Pilgrim,   See Helen Bacovcin, trans., *The Way of the Pilgrim and The Pilgrim Continues His Way* (New York: Image Books, 1978), 13.

53 *Some have called it*   See Henri Nouwen, *The Way of the Heart* (New York: Ballantine, 1981).

56 *During my first retreat*   Dom Peter McCarthy became abbot of Our Lady of Guadalupe Trappist Abbey in 1995.

64 *On the whole*   Thomas C. Oden, *Pastoral Theology: Essentials of Ministry* (New York: HarperCollins, 1983), 211–12.

64 *Oden offers several reasons*   Oden, *Pastoral Theology*, 212.

64 *"In modern society we have*   Oden, *Pastoral Theology*, 213.

65 *In a society which values*   Quoted from E.J. Dionne Jr., "A Discomfiting Message," *Oregonian* (Portland, Oregon), April 19, 2008, B4.

66 *But Thomas Oden challenges*   Oden, *Pastoral Theology*, 212.

66 *Instead of avoiding admonition*   Oden, *Pastoral Theology*, 210.

66   *"One member of the body*   Oden, *Pastoral Theology*, 210.

66   *According to Oden, the practice*   Oden, *Pastoral Theology*, 210.

73   *"For Gregory, that true artist*   R.A. Markus, *Gregory the Great and His World* (New York: Cambridge University Press, 1997), 68.

74   *"The amateur is a lover*   Margaret Guenther, *Holy Listening: The Art of Spiritual Direction* (Boston: Cowley Publications, 1992), 141.

76   *Perignon was an avid winemaker*   Karen MacNeil, *The Wine Bible* (New York: Workman, 2001), 162–63.

78   *"Play is the business*   Jeff Sigafoos, "The Wages of Playing Are Fun and Learning," *International Journal of Disability, Development and Education* 46:3 (September, 1999): 285.

79   *Children were seen as a gift*   Benedictine Oblates today are adults who have offered their lives as a gift to God, seeking to live according to the *Rule* as their station in life allows. In 2006, I became a Benedictine Oblate of Mount Angel Abbey, Mount Angel, Oregon. For more information on the life of a Benedictine Oblate, see www.osb.org/obl/index.html (accessed October 13, 2008).

80   *Cellarer in Latin is* cellararius,   Fry, *RB 1980*, 410.

81   *"The term* eucharistia   Fry, *RB 1980*, 410.

82   *"The present is the point*   C.S. Lewis, *The Screwtape Letters*, 77–78.

83   *Benedict miraculously recovered*   Gregory, *Life and Miracles*, 20.

86   *St. Benedict looks upon work*   Fry, *RB 1980*, 96.

86   *Monasteries once owned*   Gerald L. Sittser, *Water from a Deep Well: Christian Spirituality from Early Martyrs to Modern Missionaries* (Downers Grove, IL: InterVarsity Press, 2007), 97.

94   *Spiritually minded parents call*   See David Robinson, *The Busy Family's Guide to Spirituality: Practical Lessons for Modern Living from the Monastic Tradition* (New York: Crossroad, 2009).

95   *We are wise not only to ask*   For one of the most readable editions of the *Rule*, see Joan Chittister's, *The Rule of Benedict: Insights for the Ages* (New York: Crossroad, 1995). Many other excellent books on Benedictine spirituality are readily available, including Robert Benson's *A Good Life: Benedict's Guide to Everyday Joy* (Brewster, MA: Paraclete Press, 2004). Others are listed in the bibliography.

96   *Elected silence sing to me*   W.H. Gardner, ed., *Gerard Manley Hopkins: Poems and Prose* (New York: Penguin Books, 1953), 5.

101   *This act creates*   In Latin, *claustra* is defined by Timothy Fry as "any sort of space set off or closed to access by some sort of a barrier, natural or otherwise" (Fry, *RB 1980*, 289). For more ideas on the practice of the cloistered life within the family, see the author's book, *The Busy Family's Guide to Spirituality*.

102   *In the second movement*   In RB, 48.23, Benedict uses the word *meditare*, translated by *RB 1980* as "study." Benedictine scholar Terrence Kardong, OSB, writes of this practice, "For the monks of this period, *meditatio* was not the silent intellectual exercise it is for us, but rather the verbal repetition of a memorized text." See Kardong, *Benedict's Rule*, 170.

109   *Such a challenging pilgrimage*   For an excellent personal account of walking the *Camino de Santiago*, see Joyce Rupp's book *Walk in a Relaxed Manner: Life Lessons from the Camino* (Maryknoll, NY: Orbis Books, 2005).

112   *I saw a stranger today*   I first discovered this anonymous "Celtic Rune of Hospitality" on the Isle of Iona, Scotland, in September 2005.

119   *One example is*   For more information, see www.brehmcenter.com.

121   *This approach to the spiritual*   The phrase "radical hospitality" was drawn from an excellent book on Benedictine hospitality, *Radical Hospitality: Benedict's Way of Love*, by Daniel Homan, OSB, and Lonni Collins Pratt (Brewster, MA: Paraclete Press, 2002).

121   *Tracy Kidder asks*   Tracy Kidder, *Mountains Beyond Mountains: The Quest of Dr. Paul Farmer, a Man Who Would Cure the World* (New York: Random House, 2004), 296.

122   *Here I am in the middle*   Kidder, *Mountains Beyond Mountains*, 62.

122   *By seeking to fulfill*   For more information about how to get involved with Dr. Paul Farmer's organization, Partners in Health, see www.pih.org.

124   *"Never doubt that a small group*   See www.paxchristiusa.org/news_events_more.asp?id=263 (accessed April 30, 2010)

130   *"just as a tree cannot bear*   Saying XXVII from Merton, *The Wisdom of the Desert*, 34.

131   *The percentage of the American farm*   See "Urbanization of America," http://www.theusaonline.com/people/urbanization.htm (accessed June 4, 2008).

133 *Our work has found*   From a September 25, 2001, article, "A Profile of Protestant Pastors." See http://www.barna.org/barna-update/article /5-barna-update/59-a-profile-of-protestant-pastors-in-anticipation -of-qpastor-appreciation-monthq (accessed April 30, 2010).

134 *Benedictine stability is a promise*   Joan Chittister, osb, *Wisdom Distilled from the Daily: Living the Rule of St. Benedict Today* (New York: HarperCollins, 1990), 151, 156.

135 *This is the most marvelous thing*   Gregory of Nyssa, *Life of Moses* (Mahwah, NY: Paulist Press, 1978), 117–18.

136 *The second Benedictine vow*   Richard Yeo, osb, writes, "'Fidelity to monastic life' is an attempt to translate the Latin words *conversatio morum*. The meaning of this term has baffled scholars and commentators for years. One way of approaching it is to see it as the core element in the monastic commitment." See *The Benedictine Handbook* (Collegeville, MN: Liturgical Press, 2003), 123.

136 *To say that I will*   Esther de Waal, *A Life-Giving Way: A Commentary on the Rule of St. Benedict* (Collegeville, MN: Liturgical Press, 1955), 156–57.

136 *According to M. Basil Pennington,*   M. Basil Pennington, *Listen with Your Heart: Spiritual Living with the Rule of Saint Benedict* (Brewster, MA: Paraclete Press, 2007), 117.

136 *This vow of the common,*   Pennington, *Listen with Your Heart*, 117.

137 *Every other man is a piece*   Thomas Merton, *No Man Is an Island* (New York: Harcourt, Brace and Company, 1955), xxii–xxiii.

137 *When you stop and think*   de Waal, *A Life-Giving Way*, 155.

137 *"the ancients assumed*   Kardong, *Benedict's Rule*, 474.

138 *It is because I am at home*   de Waal, *A Life-Giving Way*, 158.

140 *"It is only when I remind*   de Waal, *A Life-Giving Way*, 39-40.

141 *"Insistence on concrete action*   Kardong, *Benedict's Rule*, 7.

141 *"Our postmodern worldview*   Laura Swan, osb, *Engaging Benedict: What the Rule Can Teach Us Today* (Notre Dame, IN: Ave Maria Press, 2005), 54.

142 *The early monastic approach*   Swan, *Engaging Benedict*, 54.

145 *It is the duty of elders*   Presbyterian Church (U.S.A.), *Book of Order 2007–2009: The Constitution of the Presbyterian Church (U.S.A.)*

(Louisville, KY: Office of the General Assembly, 2007), G-6.0304; G-6.0401-2.

148 *face a number of very basic*   de Waal, *A Life-Giving Way*, 55.

149 *Today, there are an estimated*   From 2005 Report from Alton Abbey, in England on the 2005 Oblates' World Congress. See http://altonabbey.org. uk/nigel/alton.nsf/All+Frame/3B6737C4756292838025711C006F7437 (accessed July 10, 2008).

149 *Formed by the Benedictine monastic*   From a plaque on the guesthouse wall of Mount Angel Abbey, Mount Angel, Oregon, from February 2008.

153 *No Christian community is more*   Dietrich Bonhoeffer, *Life Together: A Discussion of Christian Fellowship* (New York: Harper & Row, 1954), 21.

153 *"One is a brother to another*   Bonhoeffer, *Life Together*, 25.

154 *"The prayer of the Psalms,*   Bonhoeffer, *Life Together*, 73.

155 *"Sin demands to have a man*   Bonhoeffer, *Life Together*, 112.

155 *"Here the community*   Bonhoeffer, *Life Together*, 122.

155 *The restoration of the church*   Dietrich Bonhoeffer, *Testament to Freedom* (San Francisco: HarperSanFrancisco, 1997), 424.

157 *Columba founded a monastery*   For more information on the life of Columba, see Michael Mitton, *The Soul of Celtic Spirituality in the Lives of Its Saints* (Mystic, CT: Twenty-Third Publications, 1996); Ian Bradley, *The Celtic Way* (London: Darton, Longman, and Todd, 2004); and George G. Hunter III, *The Celtic Way of Evangelism* (Nashville: Abingdon Press, 2000).

158 *All of these people*   For more information on the Iona Community, visit their website at www.iona.org.uk/.

159 *"This Rule contains only*   Roger Schutz, *The Rule of Taizé* (Taizé, France: Les Presses de Taizé, 1968), 11. Today the *Rule of Taizé* is known as the "Little Source" of Taizé. See Brother Roger of Taizé, *The Sources of Taizé* (Taizé, France: Ateliers et Presses de Taizé, 2000).

160 *"The purpose of the council*   Roger Schutz, *The Rule of Taizé*, 37.

160 *Like you, pilgrims and friends*   From the Taizé Community website: http://www.taize.fr/en_article6718.html (accessed June 24, 2008). For more information regarding the Taizé Community, see their website at www.taize.fr/en.

162   *In April 2008, Dr. Ian Bradley*   From *London Independent*, April 23, 2008; http://www.independent.co.uk/news/uk/this-britain/homegrown-holy-man-cry-god-for-harry-britain-and-st-aidan-814057.html (accessed June 27, 2008).

163   *"The monastery which he established*   Bradley, *The Celtic Way*, 21. For more on the story of Aidan's life, see Michael Mitton's *The Soul of Celtic Spirituality in the Lives of Its Saints*; Ian Bradley, *The Celtic Way*; and George G. Hunter III, *The Celtic Way of Evangelism*.

163   *The Northumbria Community of England*   The Northumbria Community, *Celtic Daily Prayer: Prayers and Readings from the Northumbrian Community* (San Francisco: HarperSanFrancisco, 2002), 9.

164   *Community members meet together*   *Northumbria Community Celtic Daily Prayer*, 10. For more information on the Northumbria Community, explore their website at www.northumbriacommunity.org.

165   *In the United States, this movement*   In a February 3, 2008, article in the *Boston Globe*; "The Unexpected Monks," by Molly Worthen http://www.boston.com/bostonglobe/ideas/articles/2008/02/03/the_unexpected_monks/ (accessed July 1, 2008).

165   *The New Monasticism Gathering in 2004 agreed*   Jonathan Wilson-Hartgrove, *New Monasticism: What it has to Say to Today's Church* (Grand Rapids, MI: Brazos Press, 2008), 39. See also The Rutba House, ed., *Schools for Conversion: Twelve Marks of a New Monasticism* (Eugene, OR: Cascade, 2005).

166   *"May God give us grace*   Wilson-Hartgrove, *New Monasticism*, 39.

167   *"We are waiting not for a God*   Alasdair McIntyre, *After Virtue* (Notre Dame, IN: University of Notre Dame Press, 1984), 263; quoted from Wilson-Hartgrove, *New Monasticism*, 31.

167   *John R. Stott,*   See http://www.christianitytoday.com/ct/2005/septemberweb-only/52.0.html (accessed July 1, 2008).

173   *He picks up the pilgrimage*   Regarding the final chapter of the *Rule*, Aquinata Bockmann writes, "RB 73 is not simply the last chapter of the Rule, but rather a real epilogue explaining the purpose of the entire Rule. It is a reflection on how to observe the Rule, a kind of cover letter." Aquinata Bockmann, OSB, *Perspectives on the Rule of St. Benedict: Expanding Our Hearts in Christ* (Collegeville, MN: Liturgical Press, 2005), 77.

176 *As we heard in the Taizé community* Schutz, *The Rule of Taizé*, 11.

185 *Websites and listings showing* To find retreat centers worldwide, see the following sites: www.osb.org, offering a worldwide listing of Benedictine retreat houses; www.catholiclinks.org/retirosunitedstates.htm, a website listing Catholic retreat centers worldwide. Also, www.findthedivine.com lists seventeen hundred retreat centers worldwide, including Christian and other world religion retreat centers. Or look into www.ocso.org for Trappist Monasteries, including houses of monks and houses of nuns. In addition, the following books offer retreat center information: Jane Rubietta, *Resting Place: A Personal Guide to Spiritual Retreats* (Downers Grove, IL: InterVarsity Press, 2006); and Timothy Jones, *A Place for God: A Guide to Spiritual Retreats and Retreat Centers* (New York: Doubleday, 2000).

189 *The solitary life makes sense* Quoted from *Praying with Thomas Merton*, by Wayne Simsic (Winona, MN: Saint Mary's Press, 1994), 51.

190 *My life is a listening* Thomas Merton, *Thoughts in Solitude* (New York: Farrar, Straus & Cudahy, 1956), 74, 94.

193 *The verb used in Greek* Literally, "to intensely study": *kata*—a prepositional intensifier; and *noeo*—think or use the mind to observe or study.

204 *All along my pilgrim journey* "Close to Thee," by Fanny J. Crosby.

204 *"Toward the close of the day in the year 1874,* Fanny Crosby, retold by S. Trevena Jackson, *Fanny Crosby's Story of Ninety-Four Years* (New York: Fleming H. Revell, 1915), 79.

205 *The Road goes ever on* J.R.R. Tolkien, *The Fellowship of the Ring* (New York: Houghton Mifflin, 1954), 44.

208 *O God, the strength* *The Benedictine Handbook* (Collegeville, MN: Liturgical Press, 2003), 183–84.

210 *"O, the comfort,* Poem "Friendship" by Dinah Maria Mulock Craik, quoted from *The Best Loved Poems of the American People*, Hazel Fellerman, ed. (Garden City, NY: Garden City Books, 1936), 43.

SELECTED BIBLIOGRAPHY

Bacovcin, Helen, trans. *The Way of the Pilgrim and The Pilgrim Continues His Way*. New York: Image Books, 1978.

The Benedictine Handbook. Collegeville, MN: Liturgical Press, 2003.

Benson, Robert. *A Good Life: Benedict's Guide to Everyday Joy*. Brewster, MA: Paraclete Press, 2004.

Bockmann, Aquinata, OSB. *Perspectives on the Rule of St. Benedict: Expanding Our Hearts in Christ*. Collegeville, MN: Liturgical Press, 2005.

The Book of Common Prayer. New York: Oxford University Press, 1979.

Bonhoeffer, Dietrich. *Life Together: A Discussion of Christian Fellowship*. New York: Harper & Row, 1954.

_____. *Psalms: The Prayerbook of the Bible*. Minneapolis: Augsburg, 1970.

_____. *Testament to Freedom*. San Francisco: HarperSanFrancisco, 1997.

Bradley, Ian. *The Celtic Way*. London: Darton, Longman, and Todd, 2004.

Brooke, Christopher. *The Age of the Cloister: The Story of Monastic Life in the Middle Ages*. Mahwah, NJ: HiddenSpring, 2003.

Casey, Michael, OCSO. *Sacred Reading: The Ancient Art of* Lectio Divina. Liguori, MO: Triumph Books, 1996.

Chittister, Joan, OSB. *The Rule of Benedict: Insights for the Ages*. New York: Crossroad, 1995.

_____. *Wisdom Distilled from the Daily: Living the Rule of St. Benedict Today*. New York: HarperCollins, 1990.

de Waal, Esther. *A Life-Giving Way: A Commentary on the Rule of St. Benedict*. Collegeville, MN: Liturgical Press, 1995.

_____. *Seeking God: The Way of St. Benedict*. Collegeville, MN: Liturgical Press, 1984.

Ellsberg, Robert. *All Saints: Daily Reflections on Saints, Prophets, and Witnesses for Our Time*. New York: Crossroad, 1997.

Feiss, Hugh, OSB. *Essential Monastic Wisdom: Writings on the Contemplative Life*. San Francisco: HarperSanFrancisco, 1999.

Foster, Richard. *Life with God: Reading the Bible for Spiritual Transformation.* New York: HarperCollins, 2008.

Frend, W.H.C. *The Rise of Christianity.* Philadelphia: Fortress Press, 1985.

Fry, Timothy, ed. *RB 1980: The Rule of St. Benedict in English.* Collegeville, MN: Liturgical Press, 1982.

_____, Timothy Horner, and Imogene Baker, eds. *RB 1980: The Rule of St. Benedict in Latin and English with Notes.* Collegeville, MN: Liturgical Press, 1981.

Glenstal Abbey. *The Glenstal Book of Prayer: A Benedictine Prayer Book.* Collegeville, MN: Liturgical Press, 2001.

Gregory the Great. *Life and Miracles of St. Benedict.* Translated by Odo J. Zimmerman, OSB. Collegeville, MN: Liturgical Press, 1984.

Guenther, Margaret. *Holy Listening: The Art of Spiritual Direction.* Boston: Cowley Publications, 1992.

Herwegen, Ildephonsus, OSB. *St Benedict: A Character Study.* Translated by Dom Peter Nugent, OSB. London: Herder Books, 1924.

Homan, Daniel, OSB and Lonni Collins Pratt. *Radical Hospitality: Benedict's Way of Love.* Brewster, MA: Paraclete Press, 2002.

Hunter, George G., III. *The Celtic Way of Evangelism.* Nashville: Abingdon Press, 2000.

Jamison, Christopher, OSB. *Finding Sanctuary: Monastic Steps for Everyday Life.* Collegeville, MN: Liturgical Press, 2006.

Job, Rueben P., and Norman Shawchuck. *A Guide to Prayer for Ministers and Other Servants.* Nashville: Upper Room Books, 1983.

Kardong, Terrence G., OSB. *Benedict's Rule: A Translation and Commentary.* Collegeville, MN: Liturgical Press, 1996.

Latourette, Kenneth Scott. *A History of Christianity: Vol. 1, Beginnings to 1500.* New York: Harper & Row, 1975.

Leclercq, Jean, OSB. *The Love of Learning and the Desire for God.* Translated by Catharine Misrahi. New York: Fordham University Press, 1974.

Lewis, C.S. *Mere Christianity.* London: Garden City Press, 1952.

_____. *The Screwtape Letters.* New York: Macmillan, 1976.

MacNeil, Karen. *The Wine Bible.* New York: Workman, 2001.

Markus, R.A. *Gregory the Great and His World.* New York: Cambridge University Press, 1997.

McKnight, Scot. *Praying with the Church: Following Jesus Daily, Hourly, Today.* Brewster, MA: Paraclete Press, 2006.

Merton, Thomas. *The Asian Journal of Thomas Merton.* New York: New Directions, 1975.

_____. *No Man Is an Island.* New York: Harcourt, Brace and Company, 1955.

_____. *Thoughts in Solitude.* New York: Farrar, Straus & Cudahy, 1956.

_____. *The Wisdom of the Desert.* New York: New Directions, 1960.

Miller, J. Keith. *A Hunger for Healing: The Twelve Steps as a Classic Model for Christian Spiritual Growth.* New York: HarperCollins, 1991.

Mitton, Michael. *The Soul of Celtic Spirituality in the Lives of Its Saints.* Mystic, CT: Twenty-Third Publications, 1996.

Mullins, Edwin. *Cluny: In Search of God's Lost Empire.* New York: Blue-Bridge, 2006.

Northumbria Community. *Celtic Daily Prayer: Prayers and Readings from the Northumbria Community.* San Francisco: HarperSanFrancisco, 2002.

Nouwen, Henri J.M. *Spiritual Direction: Wisdom for the Long Walk of Faith.* New York: HarperCollins, 2006.

_____. *The Way of the Heart.* New York: Ballantine, 1981.

Oden, Thomas C. *Pastoral Theology: Essentials of Ministry.* New York: HarperCollins, 1983.

Okholm, Dennis. *Monk Habits for Everyday People: Benedictine Spirituality for Protestants.* Grand Rapids, MI: Brazos Press, 2007.

Packer, J.I. *Knowing God.* Downers Grove, IL: InterVarsity Press, 1973.

Peace, Richard. *Contemplative Bible Reading: Experiencing God Through Scripture.* Colorado Springs, CO: NavPress, 1999.

Pennington, M. Basil, OCSO. *Listen with Your Heart: Spiritual Living with the Rule of Saint Benedict.* Brewster, MA: Paraclete Press, 2007.

Peterson, Eugene. *Eat This Book: A Conversation in the Art of Spiritual Reading.* Grand Rapids, MI: Wm. B. Eerdmans, 2006.

Presbyterian Church (U.S.A.). *Book of Order 2007–2009: The Constitution of the Presbyterian Church (U.S.A.).* Louisville, KY: Office of the General Assembly, 2007.

Robbins, Maggie, and Duffy Robbins. *Enjoy the Silence: A 30 Day Experiment in Listening to God.* Brewster, MA: Paraclete Press, 2005.

Robinson, David. *The Busy Family's Guide to Spirituality: Practical Lessons for Modern Living from the Monastic Tradition.* New York: Crossroad, 2009.

Rupp, Joyce. *Walk in a Relaxed Manner: Life Lessons from the Camino.* Maryknoll, NY: Orbis Books, 2005.

The Rutba House, ed. *Schools for Conversion: Twelve Marks of a New Monasticism.* Eugene, OR: Cascade, 2005.

Schutz, Roger. *The Rule of Taizé.* Taizé, France: Les Presses de Taizé, 1968.

Sittser, Gerald L. *Water from a Deep Well: Christian Spirituality from Early Martyrs to Modern Missionaries.* Downers Grove, IL: InterVarsity Press, 2007.

Sutera, Judith, OSB, ed. *Work of God: Benedictine Prayer.* Collegeville, MN: Liturgical Press, 1997.

Swan, Laura, OSB. *Engaging Benedict: What the Rule Can Teach Us Today.* Notre Dame, IN: Ave Maria Press, 2005.

Ten Boom, Corrie. *Tramp for the Lord.* New York: Jove Books, 1978.

Thompson, Marjorie. *Soul Feast: An Invitation to the Christian Spiritual Life.* Louisville, KY: Westminster John Knox Press, 2005.

Tvedten, Brother Benet, OSB. *How to Be a Monastic and Not Leave Your Day Job: An Invitation to Oblate Life.* Brewster, MA: Paraclete Press, 2006.

Vest, Norvene, OSB. *Preferring Christ: A Devotional Commentary and Workbook on the Rule of St. Benedict.* Valyermo, CA: Ravens Press, 1990.

Wilson-Hartgrove, Jonathan. *New Monasticism: What It Has to Say to Today's Church.* Grand Rapids, MI: Brazos Press, 2008.

ABOUT PARACLETE PRESS

WHO WE ARE

Paraclete Press is a publisher of books, recordings, and DVDs on Christian spirituality. Our publishing represents a full expression of Christian belief and practice—from Catholic to Evangelical, from Protestant to Orthodox.

We are the publishing arm of the Community of Jesus, an ecumenical monastic community in the Benedictine tradition. As such, we are uniquely positioned in the marketplace without connection to a large corporation and with informal relationships to many branches and denominations of faith.

WHAT WE ARE DOING

BOOKS. Paraclete publishes books that show the richness and depth of what it means to be Christian. Although Benedictine spirituality is at the heart of all that we do, we publish books that reflect the Christian experience across many cultures, time periods, and houses of worship. We publish books that nourish the vibrant life of the church and its people—books about spiritual practice, formation, history, ideas, and customs.

We have several different series, including the best-selling Living Library, Paraclete Essentials, and Paraclete Giants series of classic texts in contemporary English; A Voice from the Monastery—men and women monastics writing about living a spiritual life today; award-winning literary faith fiction and poetry; and the Active Prayer Series that brings creativity and liveliness to any life of prayer.

RECORDINGS. From Gregorian chant to contemporary American choral works, our music recordings celebrate sacred choral music through the centuries. Paraclete distributes the recordings of the internationally acclaimed choir Gloriæ Dei Cantores, praised for their "rapt and fathomless spiritual intensity" by *American Record Guide*, and the Gloriæ Dei Cantores Schola, which specializes in the study and performance of Gregorian chant. Paraclete is also the exclusive North American distributor of the recordings of the Monastic Choir of St. Peter's Abbey in Solesmes, France, long considered to be a leading authority on Gregorian chant.

DVDS. Our DVDs offer spiritual help, healing, and biblical guidance for life issues: grief and loss, marriage, forgiveness, anger management, facing death, and spiritual formation.

LEARN MORE ABOUT US AT OUR WEBSITE:
www.paracletepress.com, or call us toll-free at 1-800-451-5006.

RADICAL HOSPITALITY
Benedict's Way of Love

Fr. Daniel Homan, osb, and Lonni Collins Pratt

ISBN: 978-1-55725-441-2 • $16.95 • Trade Paper

True Benedictine hospitality requires that we welcome the stranger, not only into our homes but into our hearts. With warmth, humor, and the wisdom of the monastic tradition, Pratt and Homan present a radical vision for a kinder world.

"A heartfelt sharing of stories, a welcome mat to enter into the spiritual discipline of hospitality." —*Publishers Weekly*

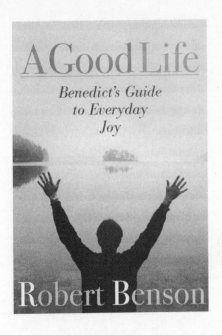

A GOOD LIFE

Benedict's Guide to Everyday Joy

Robert Benson

ISBN: 978-1-55725-449-8 • $13.95 • Trade Paper

Reflecting on what makes a "Good Life," Robert Benson offers a warmhearted guide to enriching our lives with the wisdom of Benedict. Each chapter is shaped around a Benedictine principle: prayer, rest, community, and work, and explores the timeless, practical ways that Benedictine spirituality can shape our lives today.

"Handy and insightful." —*Spirituality and Health*

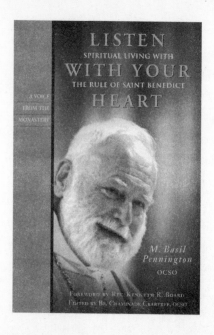

LISTEN WITH YOUR HEART

Spiritual Living with the Rule of Saint Benedict

M. Basil Pennington, OCSO

ISBN: 978-1-55725-548-8 • $15.95 • Trade Paper

"Benedict is saying, 'Wake up! Open your eyes! Open your ears! Let the divine life and light invade you so that your life is filled with aspiration, joy, and hope.'" —M. Basil Pennington

This ancient rule continues to be a guide for people of all backgrounds who desire to live a Christian life.

ALSO AVAILABLE ON 2 COMPACT DISCS
ISBN: 978-1-55725-555-6 • 155 minutes • $24.95

Available from most booksellers or through Paraclete Press:
www.paracletepress.com; 1-800-451-5006. Try your local bookstore first.